THINK AHEAD
to First Certificate

JON NAUNTON

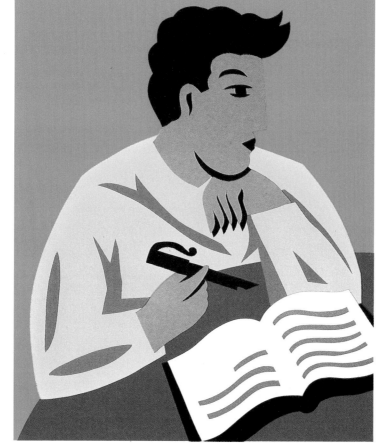

Longman

Map of the book / Contents

*[P] indicates that students have to refer to the Pairwork section on pages 136–143

The Art of Deception

SPEAKING

Fashion survey

Ask other students these questions. How far does the class agree about fashion?

1 How important is being fashionable to you?

2 Which clothes do you like wearing most?

3 Do you dress up for formal occasions?

4 Do you ever have to wear things you hate?

5 Have you ever had arguments about clothes?

6 Which brands of clothes do you prefer?

7 Which nationalities do you think are the most /least fashionable?

VOCABULARY

Clothes and fashion

1 Find the odd one out in each case. There may be more than one answer!

Example: **A** scarf **B** shawl **C** gloves

1	**A** hat	**B** cap	**C** tie		
2	**A** skirt	**B** blouse	**C** shirt		
3	**A** vest	**B** socks	**C** tights	**D** stockings	
4	**A** boots	**B** sandals	**C** belt	**D** shoes	
5	**A** jacket	**B** pullover	**C** cardigan		
6	**A** tracksuit	**B** suit	**C** trainers		
7	**A** striped	**B** purple	**C** patterned	**D** plain	**E** checked

2 In pairs, now label your dummies.

STUDENT A turn to p. 136.   STUDENT B turn to p. 140.

3 Complete the words using one letter for each space.

1 Lipstick and eye-shadow are both kinds of *m _ _ - _ .*
2 That's a very *s _ _ _ _* suit. Are you going for an interview?
3 These jeans are too *t _ _ _ _.* Have you got a bigger size?
4 I can hardly walk in these *h _ _ -h _ _ _ _* shoes.
5 Her clothes are so *o _ -f _ _ _ _ _ _ _* ; she should wear modern things.

LISTENING

Women's fashions since the 1950s

1 Look at the photographs of women in typical British fashions since the 1950s.
Which ones do you like the most/the least?

2 Listen to the short descriptions and match them with the photographs.
Which photo is missing? Can you draw the clothes?

A B C D

3 Listen again and follow the tapescript on p. 150. Underline the ways in which
the speaker:

* introduces what the women are wearing.
* gives opinions.

WRITING

Describing how someone is dressed

Study this written description of the woman dressed in the fashions of 1951. Use it
as a model and write a short description of one of your classmates; then read it out
and ask the others to guess who it is.

> She is formally dressed and looks terribly old-fashioned. She is wearing
> a matching skirt and jacket, a funny little hat, and high-heeled shoes;
> she is carrying a tiny bag. Her clothes look tight and uncomfortable.

SPEAKING

Look at the cartoon and put the speech bubbles in the right order to make a sensible conversation.

- How does Penny feel about Alex's clothes?
- Why is Alex proud of what he is wearing?
- Whose attitude do you agree with?

 READING

The fashion fraud

You are going to read about a detective agency which exposes people who copy famous goods.

1 Read the text quickly and find out who Vincent, Gerry and Miguel are.

2 Read the text again and answer these questions.

1 How do you think the writer feels about faking fashion goods?
2 What was Gerry's assignment and how do we know it was dangerous?
3 What trap did Miguel set for Gerry?

3 Word search
How many words can you find in the text which express the idea of 'authentic' and 'not authentic'?

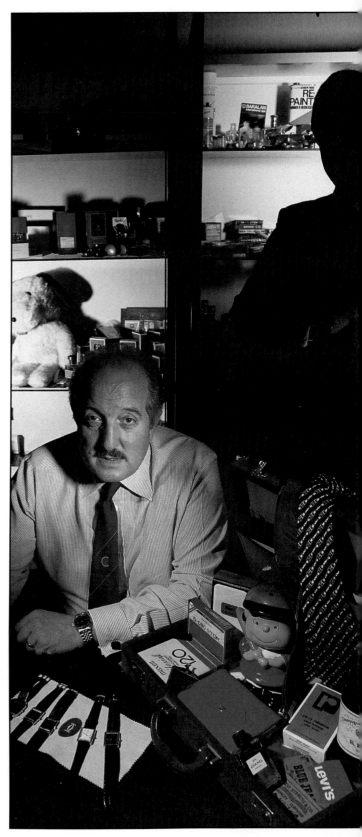

In most markets you can buy fashion goods. They may look like the real thing and carry famous labels but nearly all are fake. But does this really matter if it means we can dress fashionably but cheaply? Don't we pay far too much for fashion goods anyway? Aren't the manufacturers of the genuine articles just exploiting our ridiculous snobbery?

Understandably, they don't agree and employ investigator Vincent Carratu to find out who is making the counterfeit goods. Carratu heads his own investigation agency specializing in this kind of crime. Once he knows who the criminals are, he pretends to be a buyer. When he has enough evidence, he contacts the police.

It is a dangerous game, so Carratu takes on as his agents ex-policemen with experience of undercover work. They need to be able to act and have nerves of steel, as this example shows. One of Carratu's agents, Gerry, was asked to look into a case involving imitation whisky. Gerry pretended to be a buyer for the American Mafia and made contact with the suppliers. In the meantime, the man who had told Carratu's agency about the factory disappeared. He had almost certainly been murdered by the counterfeiters. Yet, despite the obvious dangers, Gerry continued and persuaded the gang that his story was true.

But one member, Miguel, was still suspicious and set a trap. He asked Gerry how whisky was made. Naturally, Gerry knew all about the process but realized that the kind of criminal he was playing wouldn't know. 'How should I know?' he replied. 'I just drink the stuff.' At this, Miguel relaxed. There were no more problems and Gerry obtained information which led to the arrest of the entire network. This included customs officers and policemen! At last the counterfeiters had been taken in. ∎

VOCABULARY

Phrasal verbs

1 Study these two sentences.

A *She **took** his photograph **in** the restaurant.*
B *...the counterfeiters had been **taken in**.*

In both sentences **take** appears followed by **in**. In sentence **A, in** is a preposition relating to the location. Here is another example of **take** followed by a preposition (**at**): *He **took** the photograph **at** a party.*

In sentence **B, take** and **in** belong together and express the special meaning of *to deceive or trick*. In English, many common verbs combine with prepositions and adverbs in this way to make 'phrasal verbs'.

2 Here are other phrasal verbs from the text and the unit. Match them up with their definitions on the right.

1	find out	**A**	to try to find
2	get on with	**B**	to make known a secret
3	take on	**C**	to start to employ
4	give away	**D**	to see or understand with difficulty
5	look for	**E**	to learn or discover (a fact that was hidden)
6	make out	**F**	to have a friendly relationship with

3 Decide whether the phrasal verbs in these sentences are used correctly or incorrectly.
1 He *found out* some money in the street.
2 She was *taken in* by his false promises.
3 He left home because he couldn't *get on with* his stepmother.
4 What a lovely hat! Where did you *look for* it?   ✗ *Bad !.*
5 The manager *took* him *on* because of his experience.
6 Smoking is bad for you. Why don't you *give* it *away*?
7 She *found out* that he was lying.
8 It was too dark to *make out* the sign in the distance.
9 He *got on* well *with* his parents.

4 Choose four phrasal verbs and make your own sentences.

LISTENING

Making complaints

1 Have you ever taken something back to a shop? How did you complain? Were you calm or did you get angry? Were you successful?

2 Colin is taking a sports shirt back to a store. He received it as a present. Listen for the answers to these questions:

1 What is the problem with the shirt?
2 Does he complain successfully?
3 How does he feel at the end?

ASSISTANT:	Can I help you?
COLIN:	Yes, it's ....[1] this sports shirt. I washed it the other day. The colour ran and it shrank.
ASSISTANT:	Oh dear, I see. Do you have the ....[2]?
COLIN:	I'm ....[3], but it was in one of your bags.
ASSISTANT:	I'm sorry, ...[4] without a receipt.
COLIN:	...........................[5] to the Manageress.
ASSISTANT:	Yes of course. I'll fetch her for you.
MANAGERESS:	Are you the gentleman who brought this shirt in?
COLIN:	Yes, could you change it? It's ....[6].
MANAGERESS:	Where did you get it? Did you buy it here?
COLIN:	Actually it was a present from my girlfriend. Is ....[7]?
MANAGERESS:	I'm afraid there is. You see, ...[8].
COLIN:	An imitation? Are you sure?
MANAGERESS:	I'm absolutely positive. The crocodile is even the wrong way round.
COLIN:	I don't know ....[9].
MANAGERESS:	Forget it. But if I ....[10] with my girlfriend!

3 Listen again and try to fill in the gaps in the dialogue. How does Colin introduce and support his complaint?

4 Intonation in questions 🔲
Listen to these two questions again. What do you notice about their intonation patterns?

Where did you get it?   Did you buy it here?

VOCABULARY

Damage

Complete the sentences with the words from the box, which refer to damage.

| scratched   broken   cracked   stained   torn |

1 I .... my new white blouse by spilling coffee all over it. It's ruined!
2 Oh, no! That's the third plate you've .... this week.
3 How did this book get ....? You'll have to buy another one.
4 I'm never going to lend her my records again! Can you hear where this one has been ....?
5 This cup is .... I wouldn't use it, if I were you.

SPEAKING

Making complaints

1 Use these two situations to practise complaining and dealing with complaints.

Situation 1

STUDENT A   A record you bought recently is badly scratched. You haven't got a receipt, but you buy a lot of records from the shop.

STUDENT B   You have just started working in the shop and don't know what to do. Ask about the receipt. Ask the customer to come back when the Manager is there.

Situation 2

STUDENT A   A jacket you bought for £60 is badly stained. You think that someone has already worn it! You would like to keep it but you want some money back to compensate for the damage and to pay for cleaning it.

STUDENT B   Examine the item the customer has brought back. Ask for the receipt. Apologize and work out a compromise.

2 How assertive are you? Discuss whether you would complain in these situations and what you would say.

1 You are in a restaurant. When your meal arrives, there is a hair on it.
2 You are on a train in the middle of summer. An old man gets into your carriage and shuts the window. It is extremely hot.
3 You are on a bus. Smoking is prohibited, but a man near you lights a cigarette.
4 You have been queuing in the bank for ten minutes. When it is your turn, someone says, 'Excuse me, I'm in a hurry,' and pushes in front of you.
5 You are in a café. You ordered a glass of mineral water, but when it arrives, you are sure it is ordinary water from the tap.

LANGUAGE STUDY

Tense review

Kirsten is from Sweden. She is working as an au-pair for Mr and Mrs Graham, who live in London. She is writing to her German friend, Monika, who is a shop assistant in Newcastle.

1 Quickly read Kirsten's letter and think of a suitable title for her story.

2 Go through it, putting the verbs in *italics* into a suitable form.

17 Linwood Terrace
London N8 7TW

Dear Monika,

It was so nice to hear from you again. I hope you (1) *get on* better with your boss, she (2) *sound* terrible. If I (3) *be* you I (4) *leave* and come to London. If I (5) *ask* Mrs Graham she (6) *find* an English family which (7) *need* an au-pair.

I (8) *have* a difficult time lately. You (9) *remember* my old boyfriend Victor? Well, yesterday he (10) *send* to prison for (11) *steal* money from foreign girls like us. He (12) *know* I (13) *want* be a model. He (14) *say* he (15) *have* lots of contacts in Paris. After I (16) *give* him money he (17) *buy* plane tickets he disappeared. I (18) *think* I (19) *never see* him again. Then one day, I (20) *walk* along Oxford

Street when (21) *see* him with a Japanese girl. He left, and I introduced myself to her. I (22) *tell* her my story, and at first she (23) *think* I (24) *lie* but I (25) *manage* convince her.

She (26) *tell* the police where he (27) *live* and they (28) *find* a diary full of the names of the girls he (29) *take in* already. If I (30) *know* what he (31) *be* like I (32) *never give* him a penny! I (33) *not trust* another man for a long time!

Anyway, I must go now. I (34) *pick up* the children from school in ten minutes. They (35) *finish* at 4 p.m. every day. I (36) *write* again soon. Be careful.

Love,

Kirsten

P.S. Hope you like my latest photo!

3 Search the letter and find an example of:

1 the present simple	**7** conditional sentences
2 the present continuous	**8** the passive
3 the present/past perfect	**9** reported speech
4 the past simple	**10** constructions using
5 the past continuous	• the infinitive
6 the simple future	• the gerund

Which areas do you find the most difficult?

WRITING

Opening and closing letters

1 Match suitable opening and closing expressions.

1 Dear Mum and Dad,   **A** Yours faithfully,
2 Dear Colin and Alan,   **B** Yours sincerely,
3 Dear Mr and Mrs Green, **C** With best wishes,
4 Dear Sir or Madam,   **D** Lots of love,

2 Which opening and closing expressions would you use in a letter to:

1 an old school friend?   3 a government department?
2 the head teacher of your school? 4 friends of your parents?

3 Look at Kirsten's letter and find out:

1 where she puts her address.   2 where she puts her signature.

4 Can you find any expressions which would be useful for informal letters?
Example: *It was so nice to hear from you again.*

5 Practice

In her letter, Kirsten tells Monika about her ex-boyfriend Victor. Write Monika's
reply based on the picture story.

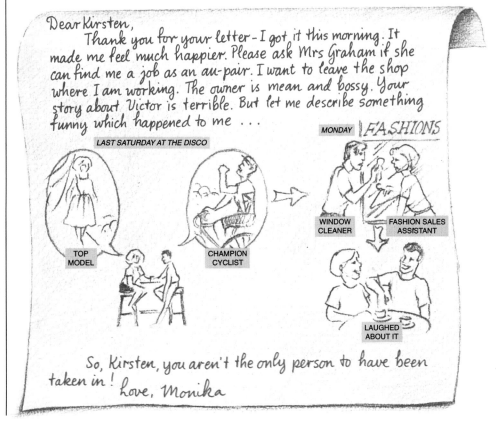

Dear Kirsten,
        Thank you for your letter – I got it this morning. It made me feel much happier. Please ask Mrs Graham if she can find me a job as an au-pair. I want to leave the shop where I am working. The owner is mean and bossy. Your story about Victor is terrible. But let me describe something funny which happened to me . . .

LAST SATURDAY AT THE DISCO

TOP MODEL

CHAMPION CYCLIST

MONDAY *FASHIONS*

WINDOW CLEANER   FASHION SALES ASSISTANT

LAUGHED ABOUT IT

So, Kirsten, you aren't the only person to have been taken in! Love, Monika

13

LISTENING

A 'Mentalist Act'

Arthur Cross, once a magician's assistant to the 'Great Marvella', is describing one of the acts they performed. Listen for the answers to these questions.

1 How did the trick work?
2 What happened if things went wrong?

LANGUAGE STUDY

After and afterwards

1 Study this example from the listening passage.

FIRST ACTION	SECOND ACTION
I put the blindfold on her.	**Afterwards**, *I went into the audience.*

2 Look at these ways of expressing the same thing.

I put the blindfold on her. I went into the audience **afterwards**.

- **After I had put** *it on her, I went into the audience.*
  After + PAST PERFECT

- **After putting** *it on her, I went into the audience.*
  After + VERB + -ing

- *I put it on her;* **after that**, *I went into the audience.*
  After that + PAST SIMPLE

WRONG: ~~I put it on her after I went into the audience.~~

It is also possible to say:
I put it on her **and** (**then**) *I went into the audience.*

3 Practice

Here are some other things the 'Great Marvella' did. Use the ways you have been shown to put them in sequence.

1 FIRST ACTION
   she ate fire

   SECOND ACTION
   she cut Arthur in half

2 FIRST ACTION
   she threw knives

   SECOND ACTION
   she caught a bullet between her teeth

WRITING

How to perform a trick

Here are Arthur's instructions for the famous trick 'How to make a rabbit appear out of a hat'.

1 Complete the text using the expressions in the box.

what you do is this   now this is the tricky bit after that   obviously   and then   first of all the following   now all you have to do

'You'll need .... ¹ for the trick: a rabbit, a chair with a solid back, a top hat and a bag held loosely together by a piece of string. .... ², put the rabbit very carefully into the bag. .... ³ hang the bag from a nail on the back of the chair. Make sure that the rabbit is comfortable and that its paws are inside the bag.
And now for the trick. .... ⁴. Invite a member of the audience up on the stage, let him examine the hat, ... ⁵ ask him to sit down on the chair. .... ⁶! As he is sitting down, pass the hat round the back of the chair, lifting the bag with the rabbit into the hat. .... ⁷, the audience will be watching the person sitting down not you! The bag will now open automatically. .... ⁸ is give the hat to your 'guest' and wait for his reaction!

2 **Giving instructions**

Look at the pictures and expand the notes to write a simple card trick.

Need an assistant. Nine cards in three rows, face down. Invite member of audience to help you. You leave room. Person chooses card, turns it over and looks at it. You come back. Ask if person has chosen a card. As you ask, watch assistant. Assistant casually places finger on any card to show position of card chosen (e.g. if top right card chosen, assistant touches top right hand corner of card). You close eyes. Think hard. Turn correct card over!

15

UNIT 2 | *Film Fantasy*

1 Look at the scenes from different types of film. Match the words with the pictures.

a western   a thriller   a cartoon   a comedy   a musical   a love story
a documentary   a horror story   an adventure   a science fiction film

2 Main stress in words 📼
Listen to the film types on tape and copy the pronunciation. Then listen again and decide in each case where the main stress is.

Example: Western Oo (Two syllables; main stress on first one.)

SPEAKING

Think of a film title for each film type.
What's your favourite type of film?
Are there any kinds of film that you can't stand?
Now find out from your classmates what their preferences are.

LISTENING

Organizing an evening out

1 Listen and find out which film Annabel, Rick and Martin decide to see and where they agree to meet.

2 Listen again and try to complete the tapescript.

ANNABEL: What ....[1] this evening?
MARTIN: ....[2] go out for a meal? ... Or maybe we ....[3] go and see a film.
RICK: I think I ....[4] go to the cinema.
ANNABEL: So would I.
MARTIN: OK. That's fine by me. ....[5]?
ANNABEL: Well, there's ....[6]. It's ....[7] science fiction thriller.
RICK: Mm, I know. It's great but I've already seen it.
MARTIN: Well, ...[8] go and see *Back to the* ....[9], then.
ANNABEL: That ....[10] a good idea. I haven't seen it yet.
RICK: ....[11] I. I really enjoyed the first two.
ANNABEL: Look. It's 6 o'clock now and the film doesn't start until 8.30. I'm going home to change.
MARTIN: ... and I'd like to get something to eat!
RICK: Me, too. Why ....[12] for a snack?
MARTIN: Thanks, that ....[13].
RICK: What about you, Annabel?
ANNABEL: Thanks for the offer, but ....[14] and change first. But I can pick you up at Rick's place in my parents' car, if I can borrow it. ....[15] 7.45 be OK?
RICK: Great. We'll see you then. ....[16] if there's a problem?
ANNABEL: I promise. See you later then. 'Bye.

3 Making suggestions and agreeing

What words and expressions are used:
● to ask for and make suggestions
● to agree with what has just been said

4 Pronunciation: don't you/could you 📼

Listen to the pronunciation of these two sentences again and practise saying them.

Why **don't⌢you** come back to my place?

Could⌢you give us a ring if there's a problem?

SPEAKING

Complete the telephone conversation between Pat and Jo using the prompts.

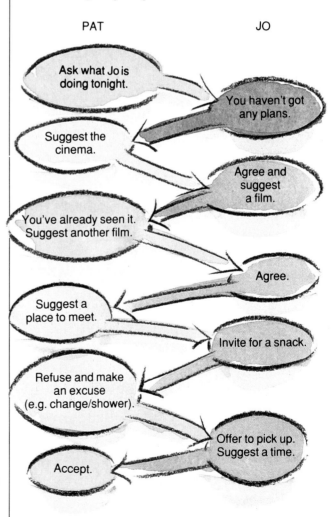

PAT

JO

Ask what Jo is doing tonight.

You haven't got any plans.

Suggest the cinema.

Agree and suggest a film.

You've already seen it. Suggest another film.

Agree.

Suggest a place to meet.

Invite for a snack.

Refuse and make an excuse (e.g. change/shower).

Offer to pick up. Suggest a time.

Accept.

READING

The nightmare man

1 Read the text about Ray Harryhausen and answer the following questions.

1 What similarities are there between fantasy films and cartoon making?
2 How many stages does Ray go through to make his models?
3 Why does he take so much trouble?
4 How did he make the fight in *The Seventh Voyage of Sinbad* look so realistic?
5 What was special about *Jason and the Argonauts*?

WRITING

Imagine that you are interviewing a film expert about Ray Harryhausen. Here are some of the answers (A). You write the questions (Q). If you need help, read the passage again to give you a context.

Q: *Could I ask you some questions about Ray Harryhausen?*
A: Of course, go ahead.
Q: ....?
A: For 35 years.
Q: ....?
A: The biggest difference is that cartoons are two-dimensional; Ray's models are three-dimensional.
Q: ....?
A: Because they don't look realistic.
Q: ....?
A: He builds them up step by step.
Q: ....?
A: 'Jason and the Argonauts'.

When we watch a fantasy film, there is often some strange and terrifying creature on the screen. There is a good chance it has been created by the artist and film-maker Ray Harryhausen. Ray has been involved in bringing our dreams and nightmares to life for the past thirty-five years. Unlike cartoonists who use just two dimensions, Ray uses all three with his models. However, both techniques share the same basic principle: small changes are made to each drawing or model before every photograph. When the shots are run together at twenty frames a second, the brain believes it is watching real action.

Ray hates artificial-looking models made from one piece, so he builds them up step by step. First of all, he makes a steel frame in order to support the body. Then he fixes the arms and legs so that they move realistically. Afterwards, the muscles are added and then the skin is stretched over them. That's why we can actually see the muscles move beneath the skin of one of his creations. Finally, the whole thing is painted. It is a long and complicated process, but

Ray feels it is worth all the trouble because, this way, he achieves the greatest realism possible.

Now the real problems start! Ray has to fit the models in with the rest of the action and scenery. This takes technical skill and clever photography. In The Seventh Voyage of Sinbad, *for example, the hero fights a skeleton swordsman. First of all, the actor playing Sinbad rehearsed the scene time and time again with an Olympic fencing champion playing his enemy. Finally, the scene was filmed with Sinbad on his own, pretending he could actually see the skeleton. It's so convincing it's hard to believe the skeleton was only added months later. However, this was child's play compared with* Jason and the Argonauts, *where there is a battle between seven skeletons and three humans! This was such a challenge that it took four months to film.*

LANGUAGE STUDY
Sequencing/Reason and purpose

1 In Unit 1, you looked at ways of putting actions into a sequence. Look again at the second paragraph of the text about Ray Harryhausen and find the words and expressions which are used for sequencing.

2 Read the paragraph once again and find the words and expressions which introduce a reason or a purpose.

3 Using the expression in brackets, re-write these sentences without changing their meaning.

Example: Chris was so nervous that she was always sick. (**because**) *She was always sick because she was so nervous.*

1 Chris went to Hollywood because she wanted to develop her career. (**that's why**)
2 She wasn't used to driving on the right; that's why she had so many accidents. (**because**)
3 She slept in car parks because she wanted to save money. (**in order to**)
4 She's studying very hard because she wants to pass the exam. (**so that**)

4 Study these two sentence patterns. When do we use **such** and when do we use **so**?
a *It was **such** a challenge **that** it took four months to film.*
b *It was **so** challenging **that** it took four months to film.*

5 Continue the second sentence so that it means the same as the one above it.

1 The film was so sad that we were miserable for the rest of the evening.
  It ....
2 He gave such a loud scream that everybody jumped out of their seats.
  His scream ....
3 It was such a funny film that she laughed until she cried.
  The film ....
4 The film was so violent that the censors banned it.
  It ....

LANGUAGE STUDY

Revision of past forms

1 There are many irregular verbs in English. Revise your knowledge of common irregular verbs by completing the table on p. 144, which includes the **infinitive**, **past simple** and **past participle** forms.
When you are sure it is correct, you can use it for reference.

2 Complete this biography of Walt Disney's early career by changing the verbs in italics into the past simple.

Walt Disney (1) *be* born on December 5th, 1901. In his teens he (2) *begin* an art course but World War I (3) *break* out and he (4) *drive* for the Red Cross in Europe. When he (5) *get* back to America he (6) *meet* the artist Ub Iwerks and they (7) *go* into business together.

They (8) *make* a series of short cartoons but (9) *lose* all their money. Luckily, Walt's brother Roy (10) *give* him more to start up again. The first talking picture (11) *come* out in 1927 and Disney (12) *see* that sound (13) *hold* the key to the future of film.

He (14) *build* on this success with other cartoons but soon (15) *feel* ready for something more ambitious. He (16) *take* the biggest risk of his career and (17) *spend* a fortune on a full-length cartoon. He finally (18) *bring* out 'Snow White' in 1935, which the public (19) *pay* millions of dollars to see. By the time he was 40, Disney and his creations (20) *be* household names around the world.

LISTENING

Three friends, Rachel, Julia and Barry, are talking about cartoon characters.

1 How has Mickey Mouse changed over the years?
Listen and make notes about his character and his appearance.
Discuss your answers with a partner.

2 Now listen again and answer the following questions.

1 Why does Rachel prefer *The Flintstones* to *Tom and Jerry*?
2 What unpleasant thing did Mickey do in his first performance?
3 How have the changes in Mickey Mouse affected viewers?

LANGUAGE STUDY

Uses of **used to**

1 Two meanings of *used to*

Rachel says: *I **used to watch** The Flintstones when I was a kid.*

         used to + VERB

Julia says: *We're not **used to** (**seeing**) that kind of **Mickey** these days.*

         used to (+ VERB + -ing)   *+ NOUN or PRONOUN*

Which sentence describes a present habit? Which one describes a past habit?

2 Pronunciation of *used to* 🔊

Listen to the two sentences again and try to copy the model. What do you notice about the pronunciation of **used to**?

3 How would you make short answers to these two questions?

- Did you use to watch *The Flintstones*? – *No, ...* .
- Are you used to watching a lot of TV? – *Yes, ...* .

SPEAKING

An interview with Chris Caine

Work in pairs.

STUDENT A   is Chris Caine, the famous Hollywood movie star (turn to p. 136).

STUDENT B   is a journalist from *Mondo Movie* magazine (turn to p. 140).

WRITING

A magazine article

Write an article about Chris Caine for *Mondo Movie* magazine. Try to include the different uses of **used to** which have been introduced. Begin the article like this:

Last month I had the enormous pleasure of interviewing Chris Caine by the poolside of the star's luxurious home in Beverley Hills. I learned some secrets about this great Hollywood star's life which are exclusive to the readers of Mondo Movie magazine.

READING | Describing a film

1 Gary Boorman is on a TV show talking about classic films from the 1980s. Read what he says and match the picture with the right part of the text.

2 Complete the text by using: **when, who, whose, why, which** and **where**. Which of these words are used to replace: people, things and animals, times, places and reasons?

'One of my favourite films is *Back to the Future*, (1) .... stars Michael J Fox. It's a kind of comedy adventure and science fiction film, (2) .... is set in a small town in the US. It opens in a house in the suburbs, (3) .... the **hero**, Marty McFly, lives with his family.

Marty's father, George, is a silly man (4) .... laughs at old TV comedies, his mother, (5) .... name is Lorraine, is dull and unattractive and a terrible housewife. The **villain** of the film is George's boss Biff, (6) .... is used to pushing him around. The other main **character** is Dr Emmett Brown, (7) .... has invented a time machine (8) .... is made from an old sports car. Dr Brown has a dog (9) .... is called Einstein.

Marty gets into the car and, by accident, is transported back to 1955, the year (10) .... his parents fell in love. He meets his father George,

(11) .... is still being bullied by Biff. However, Marty fights Biff and his gang and makes fools of them. He also meets his mother, (12) .... used to be slim and beautiful. George is madly in love with her and would like to take her to the college dance, but he is such an idiot that no girl will take him seriously.

Marty finds a photograph he has brought from the future and notices that his brother and sister are starting to disappear. This is (13) .... he has to make sure that his parents really do get together; otherwise he won't be born!

The rest of the film revolves around how he can bring them together at the dance (14) .... they are supposed to fall in love. I won't say anything else because I don't want to spoil it for you if you haven't seen it. All I will say is that the **plot** is clever, the **script** is funny and the acting and special effects brilliant. I highly recommend it to you.'

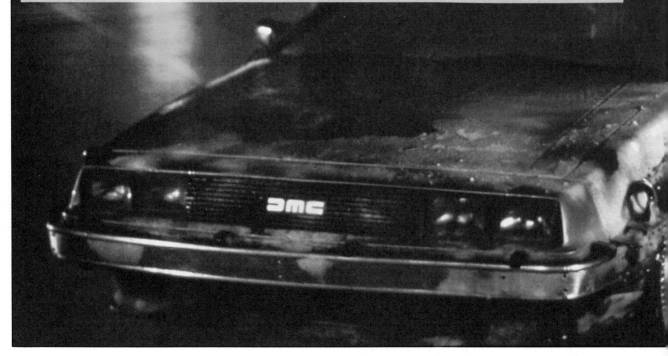

3 Word search

Which of the words highlighted in **bold** type in the text means:

- the story.
- a person in the story played by an actor.
- where (and when) the story happens.
- the 'good guy'.
- the 'bad guy'.

4

You are going to describe your favourite film. First of all, use the description of *Back to the Future* as a model and make notes about:

- the name of your favourite film
- the stars
- the kind of film
- where/when it is set
- the characters (e.g. the hero/heroine/villain)
- the plot

Which tense are you mostly going to use to describe what happens?

WRITING PREPARATION

Punctuation

1

Study these sentences and correct the punctuation where necessary.

1 When Walt Disney died he was very rich, but had known great poverty.
2 Humphrey Bogart made many films, he starred in *Casablanca*.
3 Having worked as an actor, Ronald Reagan became a politician.
4 Orson Welles directed *Citizen Kane*, it is considered the greatest film of all time.
5 We went to the cinema and had dinner at a restaurant afterwards.
6 I admire Woody Allen, I think he is a great director.
7 My son loves *The Flintstones*, they really make him laugh.
8 I love horror films but my wife prefers westerns.

2

Read the passage and add full stops where necessary.

Back to the Future III continues where part II ended Doc Brown has arrived in the American West in 1885 and Marty McFly cannot escape from 1955 they finally find each other and Marty takes the name Clint Eastwood he gets involved in train hi-jacking and a gun-fight with 'Mad Dog' Tannen the film is full of superb special effects it is an excellent conclusion to all the storylines of the three ***Back to the Future*** films

UNIT 3 | *Great Escapes*

Here are some exciting scenes from the film *Raiders of the Lost Ark*. Working in pairs or small groups, decide on a sensible order for the scenes and then describe what happens and how Indiana Jones escapes.

LANGUAGE
STUDY

Prepositions of position and direction

1 Study these prepositions and the illustrations showing their meaning.

2 Revise prepositions of position and direction by completing the text on p. 145.

3 Complete this paragraph by deciding which preposition is right in each case.

It was exactly four o'clock when she woke up. She jumped quickly (1) *outside/out* of bed, got dressed and looked (2) *across/through* the window. It was a cold winter's day and snow lay (3) *at/on* the ground. She then took her best clothes (4) *out of/off* her wardrobe and put them (5) *onto/into* her small, dusty old suitcase which was leaning (6) *onto/against* the wall. She took the money which she kept (7) *inside/into* an empty chocolate box hidden (8) *between/against/among* the wardrobe and the wall and put it (9) *to/into* her pocket. She took a note for her parents (10) *out/out of/outside* a drawer and placed it (11) *into/onto* her dressing table. Carefully, she opened the door and crept (12) *by/along* the corridor, (13) *past/behind* her parents' room and (14) *along/down* the dark staircase (15) *onto/into* the hall. She made her way (16) *at/into/towards* the back door and opened it. Closing it quietly (17) *in front of/behind* her, she moved silently (18) *through/across/down* the garden and climbed (19) *under/over/through* the low garden gate. For a few seconds, she stood (20) *from/at/on* the gate and looked back at the sleeping house. Then she turned and walked quickly away to begin a new life.

READING | She's leaving home 🔊

Read the completed text, listen to the song and think about these questions.

1 Why is the girl leaving home?
2 Do you think she feels guilty?
3 How old do you think she is?
4 Where is she going?
5 How do her parents react?
6 Do they think they have been good parents?

READING
A bowl of macaroni

1 Read the first paragraph of the text and find out why Casanova is in prison.

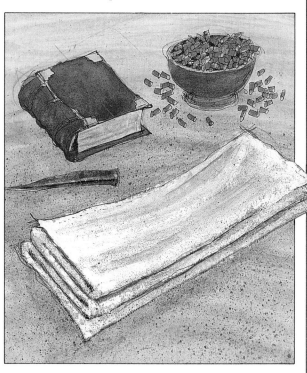

2 Look at the objects above and imagine how they helped him escape. Then read the text to check your answers.

3 Read the text again and try to imagine his escape route.

4 Word search

The writer of the text uses certain adjectives and verbs which add to the drama of the escape. Find the words that mean:

Para. 1 famous in a bad way
Para. 2 very angry
Para. 4 clever like a fox
         to move something to another place illegally
Para. 5 to move along on your hands and knees
         to walk slowly and silently to avoid detection
Para. 6 to look very closely
         to walk purposefully, with big steps

Giovanni Giacomo Casanova, history's greatest lover, was extremely nervous. He wasn't waiting for his latest conquest or hiding from an angry husband. Instead he was waiting for the beginning of his greatest adventure: escape from a notorious Venetian prison. In his youth he had written a book which attacked the church. This gave his many enemies an excellent excuse for arresting him and locking him up. Now, fifteen months later, he was ready to win back his freedom . . .

From the very beginning, Casanova had been determined to escape. He managed to get a piece of iron which he sharpened into a spike, which he then used to dig a hole in his cell floor. Just when he was about to make his attempt, he was moved to another cell. Inevitably, his furious jailer discovered the hole, but somehow Casanova managed to keep him quiet.

Casanova realized there would be no further opportunity of tunnelling his way out, as his new cell was now regularly searched. Casanova was still determined to escape, but realized he would have to involve someone else in his plans. This person was a monk called Balbi, a prisoner in the cell next door. They managed to plan their escape via messages written in invisible ink made from fruit juice.

One day Casanova asked the jailer to deliver a huge bible to Balbi as a present, together with a large dish of macaroni. The jailer was so busy trying not to spill the macaroni that he didn't notice how heavy the Bible was. The crafty Casanova had managed to smuggle the spike hidden in the book's cover!

Now the waiting was over. On the night of October 31st, 1756, Casanova saw Balbi's hand appear through a hole in the ceiling. The monk had cut through the ceiling of his own cell, crawled along the attic, then made a hole in Casanova's ceiling. Balbi now pulled Casanova up beside him. Together, they succeeded in lifting one of the heavy lead roof-tiles and, with the help of a rope made of knotted bedsheets, crept along the moonlit rooftops looking for a way down. By chance, they came across a window which led directly into the empty Palace.

Casanova changed into a suit of elegant clothes he had brought with him. Unfortunately, as he peered out of one of the windows, somebody from

below noticed him. A palace keeper unlocked the main door to find out what was going on. Realizing this was their only chance of escape, Casanova and Balbi strode past him and made for the waterfront, where they got a gondola to freedom. Casanova claims that he spent his first night hiding in the Chief of Police's house while the poor man was out searching for Casanova!

LANGUAGE STUDY
The infinitive and the gerund

*Casanova **managed to keep** him quiet.*
*... they **succeeded in lifting** one of the roof-tiles.*

1 Study the two lists of common verbs. The ones in the first list always take the infinitive and those in the second always take the gerund.

Infinitive: manage, pretend, offer, promise, hope, plan

Gerund: succeed in, consider, deny, look forward to, avoid, risk

2 Now use one of these verbs in the correct form to complete each of the following sentences.

1 She finally .... to escape by stealing a key.
2 He .... to carry the old man's suitcase.
3 I've never been to France before. I'm .... going there next year.
4 They .... reaching the frontier the following day.
5 She realized that she .... breaking a leg if she jumped from the window, but she knew there was no other choice.
6 Her mother made her .... to write home every week.
7 It was nice to see you. I .... to see you again soon.
8 When he gets out of prison, he .... to travel.
9 I would like you to .... working for me.
10 He .... stealing the car, although a witness saw him.
11 Give up smoking if you want to .... getting a cough.
12 He .... to be asleep, but in fact he heard everything they said.

VOCABULARY

Phrasal verbs

1 In the listening exercise on p. 29, you will hear six new phrasal verbs. They are in **bold** type in this paragraph. From their context, work out which ones mean:

to leave	to recover consciousness	to finish
to arrive	to begin suddenly	to escape

War had **broken out** in the desert kingdom and we realized that we had to **get away**. Amanda **turned up** at my apartment three hours late, so we immediately got the car and **set off** across the desert. Soon, our petrol supply **ran out**, but we managed to beg some from a passing lorry. We were within sight of the border, when there was a sudden loud bang and everything went black. When I **came to**, night had fallen and Amanda was watching over me with a worried expression. It was then that I realized we had driven over a land mine.

2 Complete these sentences by using each phrasal verb once.

1 He is still unconscious; I'll call you when he ....
2 She was so unhappy at home that she just had to ....
3 If you .... late, you won't be allowed into the concert.
4 We'll have to .... really early to catch the ferry.
5 Just use a cheque if your cash ....
6 A flu epidemic has .... at work; I hope I don't catch it.

LANGUAGE STUDY

Subjects, verbs and objects

English verbs are transitive, intransitive or both transitive and intransitive. A transitive verb *must* take a direct object.

Example: *We*   ***got***   ***the car****.*
            SUBJECT   VERB   OBJECT

Get is a transitive verb, so *We got.* by itself is wrong.

Fall is an intransitive verb, so we can say: *Night had fallen.*

Drive is transitive and intransitive, so we can say:
We drove the car. and *We drove over a land mine.*

We cannot use intransitive verbs in the passive.

The phrasal verbs you have just looked at are all intransitive.

LISTENING | A narrow escape

1 Key words

The words in the box will help you understand the listening text. In what kind of context would you expect to find words like these?

> protest   troublemaker   shield   stadium
> exit   police   confusion   violence   riot

2 In pairs or small groups find out:

- if anyone ever goes to pop concerts.
- if pop concerts are good value for money.
- if pop concerts can ever be dangerous.

3 Listen once to get the main points.
Whose fault do you think the riot was?

4 Listen again and decide whether these statements are **true** or **false**.

1 Janice was on holiday.
2 The concert was outside.
3 Some people were protesting about the price of entertainment.
4 All the empty seats were taken.   *Not clear*
5 The riot police had been at the stadium from the beginning.
6 The riot police blocked off every exit.
7 Some of the audience had come prepared for a fight.
8 The riot police started the violence.
9 Janice was hurt.
10 Janice couldn't understand what one of the policemen said.

5 Speaking

In pairs or small groups, discuss:

- whether you believe Janice's version of the story.
- what you think a representative from the police would say.
- whether this type of event has ever taken place in your country.

29

SPEAKING | The Wall

1 Until the Berlin Wall came down, many East Germans tried to escape into the West. In pairs or small groups, look at the photographs and discuss how people may have succeeded in escaping.

2 Since German Unification, Berlin has become a destination for 'weekend escapes'. Look at the brochure and, in groups, work out a plan of how you would spend a weekend there, arriving on Friday evening and leaving on Sunday evening.

● **SIGHTSEEING** You should visit the **Brandenburg Gate**, so long cut off from the West. If you like wildlife, visit **the world's biggest zoo** in the **Tiergarten Park**. No visit to Berlin would be complete without going through **Checkpoint Charlie**, where people used to pass from East to West. You'll also find there the **Little House**, a museum dedicated to those who have escaped from the East. **Charlottenburg Palace** is a very fine example of Baroque architecture, and there are many fascinating museums and art galleries.

● **EATING OUT** Berlin offers everything, from, Greek and Turkish cuisine to Italian, Indian and Balkan. Coffee and cakes – *Kaffee und Kuchen* – are a must!

● **SHOPPING** For shopping, visit Berlin's magnificent Kurfürstendamm. Bargain-hunters can spend hours exploring the city's fascinating flea-markets and numerous antique and second-hand bookshops.

● **NIGHTLIFE** After hard day's shopping, what better than one of Berlin's night spots? Those near the Kurfürstendamm are quite pricey but there are cheaper ones in Kreuzberg and Schöneberg.

LISTENING

Booking by telephone

Mrs Roberts is telephoning a travel agent to ask about a weekend break in Berlin.

1 Listen to Part A of the conversation. Imagine you are the telephonist. Write a short note that you would leave for a colleague.

2 Listen again and answer these questions.

1 How does Mrs Roberts tell the telephonist what she wants to know?
2 How does the telephonist
   a ask Mrs Roberts to wait?
   b ask Mrs Roberts for her name and telephone number?
   c tell Mrs Roberts someone will call her?

3 Listen to Part B of the conversation and correct Mrs Roberts' notes.

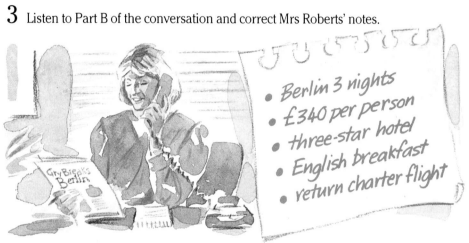

- Berlin 3 nights
- £340 per person
- three-star hotel
- English breakfast
- return charter flight

4 Listen to Part B again and answer these questions.

1 How does Sharon:
   a introduce herself?
   b show that she is trying to find the information for Mrs Roberts?
2 How does Mrs Roberts:
   a show she is pleased that Sharon has returned her call?
   b ask for information?
   c show that she is happy with the information Sharon gives her?

SPEAKING

Booking a hotel

Work in pairs.

STUDENT A   You are a receptionist at the Avonbury Hotel. Study the details on p. 137.

STUDENT B   You are ringing the Avonbury Hotel to find out some information and book a room there. Study the details on p. 141.

Now act out the telephone conversation. (Your answers to exercises 2 and 4 above will help you.)

WRITING PREPARATION

Narrative composition

Carefully study this model narrative composition and the tenses used in each paragraph.

I shall never forget the New Year's Eve party at The Stellar Hotel as long as I live. We had gone there to meet a group of special friends I had known since school. When Paul and I finally turned up at three o'clock, we went straight to the discotheque in the basement. Everybody was dancing and having a marvellous time. Paul had proposed to me at midnight and my friends were delighted to hear the news. They congratulated us and admired the beautiful ring he had given me.

Paul was buying drinks at the bar, when disaster struck. Some stupid boys were playing with cigarette lighters when suddenly some of the decorations caught fire. Within seconds, a fire broke out and spread to lots of gas-filled balloons, which started to explode. Within seconds, the ceiling was on fire and the disco filled with thick green poisonous smoke. Someone managed to get hold of a fire-extinguisher but, by now, there was no possibility of putting it out. Everybody panicked and started coughing and screaming and then the lights went out. I never saw Paul again.

How did the writer of the story escape? Think of an ending to the story and compare your ideas with your classmates.

 LANGUAGE STUDY

Narrative tenses 1

1 The past simple and past continuous

The model composition shows how the PAST CONTINUOUS is used to:

- set the scene. *Everybody was dancing and having a marvellous time. (ll. 8–10)*
- describe how a long action is interrupted by a single action or event. *Paul was buying drinks at the bar, when disaster struck. (ll. 15–16)*

Put the verbs in bold type in these sentences into the most suitable of these two tenses.

1 The guard **enter** the cell as he **dig** the tunnel.
2 When they **find** her she **cut** a hole in the fence.
3 He **arrive** while I **try** to phone him.
4 I **walk** in the woods when I **hear** a shot.
5 He **fall** over as he **cross** the road.

Look at the completed sentences and decide when, generally speaking, we use **while**, **when** and **as**.

2 The past simple and past perfect

When we describe completed actions in their obvious order, then we use the PAST SIMPLE.

Within seconds, a fire broke out and spread to lots of gas-filled balloons, which started to explode. (ll. 19–22)

In the model composition, the *past perfect* is used to describe things that happened before the main narrative or before a certain point in the past.

Paul had proposed to me at midnight. (ll. 10–11)

Decide if the *past perfect* is used correctly or incorrectly in these sentences.

1 They discovered the tunnel he had dug.
2 After she had crossed the border, she threw away her false papers.
3 He climbed down the rope and had disappeared into the trees.
4 She collected the gun she had left at the cottage.
5 We got dressed, washed and had eaten breakfast.

Look back at the story of Casanova's escape. Which tenses are used and why?

SPEAKING

Collective story telling

Imagine you are telling the story of how you were kidnapped and your escape from the kidnappers. Working in groups, look at the cues below and take it in turns to add something new to the story, and make notes as the story develops.

 WRITING

Narrative composition

Use the notes you have made in your groups and write your own story about how you escaped from the kidnappers.

When you have finished, compare your story with the others in your group.

 1 Say who you are and why you were kidnapped.
 2 Describe your journey to school/work.
 3 Describe the car that was waiting at the corner.
 4 Describe how the masked drivers got you into the car.
 5 Say how it felt when they put a bag over your head.
 6 Describe what the journey felt like and how long it took.
 7 Say how you knew you were on a farm.
 8 Describe the cellar where they put you.
 9 Describe what the two kidnappers looked like without their masks.
10 Describe how you found a hole in the roof and tried to escape.
11 Describe what happened when they caught you.
12 Describe the tape recording you had to make for your family.
13 Explain how you heard the conversation where they decided to kill you.
14 Describe how you set fire to the house and escaped.
15 Describe how the woman with the gun fell into the well.
16 Describe your escape by bicycle.
17 Describe the chase and how the second kidnapper crashed his car.
18 Say what happened when the police found you.

UNIT 4 | *Treasure*

Spot the difference

Work in pairs. Compare the two pictures and find ten differences. What is their connection with treasure?

LANGUAGE
STUDY

Countable and uncountable

Study this diagram and the explanations. Then do the exercise opposite.

How many? (use with countable nouns)		**How much?** (use with uncountable nouns)
	every/all all all	
	most most	
many, lots of, a lot of		much, lots of, a lot of
	some/several some	
not many, only a few, few		a little, not much, little
not ... any, no, none	none	not ... any, no, none

34

Rose is on the beach talking to Stan, who is using a metal detector to find 'treasure'. Decide which choices can complete the sentences. Often there is more than one correct answer.

ROSE: Hi! What are you doing?

STAN: I'm looking for **1 A** *some treasure.* **B** *a treasure.* **C** *treasure.*

ROSE: And how **2 A** *much* **B** *many* luck have you had so far?

STAN: Well, **3 A** *few* **B** *a little* **C** *little.* I've found **4 A** *some* **B** *few* **C** *a few* coins and **5 A** *much* **B** *many* **C** *lots of* **D** *a lot of* silver paper from chocolate bars and cigarette packets!

ROSE: But surely you usually find **6 A** *anything* **B** *something* valuable **7 A** *all* **B** *most* **C** *every* day.

STAN: It depends. Last Monday and Tuesday, I looked **8 A** *anywhere* **B** *everywhere* **C** *nowhere* and found absolutely **9 A** *nothing* **B** *anything* **C** *none* at all.

ROSE: Perhaps **10 A** *someone* **B** *anyone* else had been looking, too.

STAN: Maybe, but there isn't really **11 A** *much* **B** *many* competition. Nearly **12 A** *all* **B** *each* **C** *every* the enthusiasts who start give up. Only **13 A** *few* **B** *a few* come regularly enough to become experts, but they waste **14 A** *much* **B** *many* **C** *lots of* time looking in impossible places. They give up when they don't have **15 A** *an instant* **B** *any instant* **C** *instant* success.

ROSE: What's the most valuable thing you've found?

STAN: I've found **16 A** *few* **B** *a little* **C** *a few* rings and bracelets, but I always hand them in to the police.

ROSE: And do you need **17 A** *special* **B** *any special* **C** *the special* **D** *a special* equipment?

STAN: Well, only **18 A** *one metal detector* **B** *a metal detector* **C** *metal detector* like this, **19 A** *some trousers* **B** *trousers* **C** *a trousers* and **20 A** *a pair* **B** *some pair* **C** *pair* of plastic shoes.

ROSE: Where can I get **21 A** *an information* **B** *the information* **C** *some information* about it?

STAN: Buy me **22 A** *some coffee* **B** *coffee* **C** *a coffee* and I'll tell you more!

READING

The history of Captain William Kidd

1 Read the text about the pirate William Kidd and decide whether these statements are **true** or **false**.

1 Kidd was a rough and uncultured man.
2 A 'Privateer' was a pirate who had the support of his government.
3 Kidd became a sort of 'policeman'.
4 Difficult circumstances forced Kidd to become a real pirate.
5 If he had said where the treasure was hidden, he wouldn't have been executed.
6 Kidd's friends tried to save him.
7 One map shows the location of Kidd's treasure.
8 People are still searching for the treasure.

One of the .... (1) interesting characters from the days of pirates was Captain William Kidd, who has been the model for romantic tales of adventure on .... (2) oceans. He served in the Royal Navy and went on to become a successful merchant. He married a .... (3) American widow and was a gentleman with friends in high places, ... (4) than the usual rough sailor. Afterwards, for .... (5) years, he was a 'Privateer' – a sort of pirate who has a licence .... (6) his government to attack enemy merchant shipping.

Later on, he was employed by the government to destroy real pirates who .... (7) causing problems in the Caribbean. Unfortunately for Kidd, he had such .... (8) success that it forced .... (9) to turn to piracy as well. He captured a .... (10) ships but eventually he was arrested and taken .... (11) to England for trial. He was sentenced to death by Parliament. However, the day before his execution, he offered to say where .... (12) his treasure was if his life was spared. It made .... (13) difference; the judge turned his offer down and he was hanged .... (14) 23rd May 1701. His friends refused to help him.

But this .... (15) of buried treasure caught the public's imagination and, ever since then, ... (16) searches have been made for Kidd's treasure. In 1929 a man called Palmer came across a map in a desk which, it was claimed, had .... (17) belonged to Kidd. Other articles he .... (18) contained further maps giving evidence that .... (19) 'Treasure Island' really does exist. Nevertheless, so far, ... (20) has discovered it or its treasure, either.

2 Complete the text opposite using the words in the box. Sometimes, there is more than one possibility.

nobody	the	all	once	no	from	many	little	perhaps	several
few	most	rich	him	back	idea	were	on	rather	discovered

LISTENING

Sunken treasure

Francis Gosling is an expert on treasure exploration. Listen for the information which answers these questions.

1 What advice does he have for treasure hunters?
2 According to Francis, where is most treasure to be found?
3 What are the big problems associated with treasure hunting?
4 What was the 'Geldermalsen's cargo'?
5 Why was it in such good condition?
6 Who discovered 'La Nuestra Señora de Atocha'?
7 How long did the search take him?
8 How much is the cargo of the 'Admiral Nakhimov' worth?

VOCABULARY

Phrasal verbs

1 Look at these sentences from this Unit and decide which definition goes with which phrasal verb.

1 A man called Palmer came across a map in a desk. **a** to try to find
2 ... they didn't want to give the wreck's position away. **b** see with difficulty
3 Other teams had licences to look for the wreck as well. **c** tell a secret
4 We can just make out the manufacturer's name. **d** find by chance

2 All four phrasal verbs are transitive, and so they must take an object. Grammatically, there are important differences. Study the sentences.

(i) He came across a map. CORRECT   (iii) He came a map across. WRONG
(ii) He came across it.   CORRECT   (iv) He came it across.   WRONG

● With **come across** we cannot separate the verb **come** from its particle **across**. **Come across** is an *inseparable* phrasal verb.

(i) We made out the name. CORRECT   (iii) We made the name out. CORRECT
(ii) We made out it.   WRONG   (iv) We made it out.   CORRECT

● We can follow the phrasal verb with a full object (i). We can also separate the verb **make** from its particle **out** with the full object (iii) or object pronoun (iv). However, we cannot place the object pronoun ('it') after the particle (ii). **Make out** is a *separable* phrasal verb.

37

READING | Shipwreck!

1 The people in the boat have just escaped from a shipwreck. What is happening in the picture?

As well as dangers at sea, sailors used to face danger on land too. When a ship hit rocks on the coasts of Devon or Cornwall, any survivors were usually murdered. With no witnesses, local people could keep the cargo the ship had been carrying. In bad weather, wreckers even used 'Judas lights' to make sailors steer their ships onto the rocks. By the time captains realized they weren't the welcoming lights of a safe harbour, few were able to turn back.

In October 1707, the 'Association' and four other ships were sailing to England, when they were shipwrecked off the Scilly Isles. The 'Association' had been carrying a three-million-dollar cargo of silver. The admiral in charge, Sir Cloudsley Shovell, had believed he was near France and had even hanged a sailor who suggested he might be wrong!

Despite the poor man's warning, Shovell kept on his course. This was a terrible error, which cost the lives of two thousand men. A few, including Shovell, reached the shore. Although he escaped drowning, he was murdered by local women who then stole his rings and jewellery.

For a short time, the rock where the 'Association' sank was known as 'Shovell Rock'. Later, local people changed the name because they didn't want to give the wreck's position away.

Finally, in 1967, the British Royal Navy located the 'Association' and started diving, but other private teams had licences to look for it as well. Under English law, at least half of any of the silver which private teams recovered would have to be given to the government.

However, they only rescued a third of the treasure. The rest either still lies at the bottom of the sea, or else was secretly recovered over the years.

2 Read the text carefully and make questions for these answers

1 Things like storms, enemy warships and pirates.
2 He got his position wrong.
3 I think he must have been cruel and stubborn.
4 They wanted to keep the wreck's position a secret.
5 It may still be there, or else was secretly recovered.

LANGUAGE STUDY

Despite and although

1 **Despite** and **although** both show a contrast of two ideas in a sentence.

The man warned him, but Shovell kept on his course. =
***Despite** (hearing) the poor man's warning, Shovell kept on his course.*
Despite + (GERUND +) NOUN/NOUN PHRASE

He escaped drowning, but he was murdered. =
***Although** he escaped drowning, he was murdered.*
Although + VERB PHRASE

2 Make sentences using **although** and **despite** based on these details about the career of William Kidd.

1 He was a gentleman, but he became a pirate.
2 He offered to say where his treasure was, but he was hanged.
3 He had important friends, but they refused to help him.
4 There are maps of Kidd's 'Treasure Island', but nobody has found it.

Narrative tenses 2

1 Match these three sentences with the 'explanations' below.

1 When Frank arrived, Sue was drawing the map.
2 When Frank arrived, Sue drew the map.
3 When Frank arrived, Sue had drawn the map.

a Frank arrived to find that the map was ready.
b Frank arrived to find Sue busy at work on the map.
c Frank arrived and Sue began to draw the map.

2 The second paragraph of the text about the 'Association' was based around these notes. Why are different tenses used in the text?

> *The Association – 3 million dollar cargo of silver. On way to England – Admiral Sir Cloudsley Shovell gets position wrong – sailor gives warning but Shovell hangs him – ship wrecked off Scilly Isles. Shovell reaches shore. Women murder him for jewellery.*

WRITING

The Vikings are coming!

1 You are going to write a treasure story using pictures in the back of the book.

Work in pairs.   **STUDENT A**   turn to p. 137.   **STUDENT B**   turn to p. 141.

2 Now write the story in the past, using a range of narrative tenses.

VOCABULARY
Personal treasures

1 Match the names in the box with the objects.

2 Compound nouns

The noun 'candlestick' is made up of two nouns with the main stress on the first. Pick out similar words from the list and practise saying them.

3 Shapes and characteristics

Look at the objects again. Which ones are: *shiny, smooth, rough, heavy, light, worn, sharp, round, curved, oval, rectangular, pointed, spiral*? Which ones would be made of: *wood, china, metal, cloth or glass*?

LISTENING
Treasure in our attic

1 Before you listen, how much do you think each of these objects is worth? Imagine you have £5,000. How much would you bid for each one?

1 Teddy
  a nothing
  b £5
  c £50
  d £500
  e £1.000

2 Golf ball
  a nothing
  b £25
  c £50
  d £500
  e £4,000

3 Charlie Chaplin
  a nothing
  b £10
  c £100
  d £1,000
  e £2,000

4 Beatles' record
  a nothing
  b £10
  c £100
  d £1,000
  e £5,000

2 Listen again and answer these questions.

1 Where did Robin get his teddy?
2 Where was it from and who made it?
3 Where did the man find the golf ball?
4 What was wrong with it?
5 How much did the man pay for Charlie Chaplin?
6 Did he get a bargain?
7 What is special about the Beatles' record?
8 How did the girl's father get it?

golf ball   corkscrew   teddy bear
tennis racket   record   teapot
sea-chest   vase   sword   radio
porcelain figure   record-player
whistle   fan   silver candlestick

LANGUAGE STUDY

Indirect questions

1 Look at these three questions from the recording. How is **a** different in structure from **b** and **c**?

a What have you brought to show us?
b Could you tell me where he was from?
c Do you know what it's worth?

2 Intonation in questions

Questions **b** and **c** are *indirect* questions. We often use them when we want to be polite.
Listen again and try to copy the intonation of all three as closely as you can.

3 Sentences beginning with **I wonder** and **I'm not sure** look like indirect questions in their structure.

*I **wonder** where Alice is.* (Where is Alice?)
***I'm not sure** if this is the house.* (Is this the house?)

4 There is another tricky indirect question on the recording.

George Brown asks:
Would you mind telling me how much you paid for it?
Would you mind + VERB + -ing

The man answers:
Not really, I suppose. It cost me £90.
Notice that the reply **not really** means **OK.** Can you think why?
What would the man have said if he hadn't wanted to tell George the price?

5 Look at these sentences and decide if they are right or wrong. Where necessary, correct them.

1 Could you tell me what time is it?
2 I wonder what they are doing.
3 Do you know when does the train leave?
4 I'm not sure where does he work.
5 Does Marion know where the money is?
6 Could you tell me if the manager is here today?
7 Would you mind to tell me where she lives?

LANGUAGE STUDY

Adjective order

When we have more than one adjective, we tend to follow this order:
size – shape – age – material – origin – NOUN.
Put the following into the correct order.

1 square/silk/scarf
2 British/old/coin
3 bowl/wooden/round
4 large/leather/football
5 curved/vase/modern

WRITING

A treasured souvenir

Study this description of a favourite object and write one of your own.

Introduction —My favourite object is this little Russian tray.

Description/How long you have had it —It's round and rather scratched and I have had it for years. I know it's not at all valuable, but to me it's absolutely priceless.

Who gave it to you or how you got it —It was given to me by a remarkable old Russian lady. When I was little, I used to spend hours with her listening to her tales of life just after the Revolution.

Related events —She always used to serve us glasses of lemon tea from a round metal samovar. She gave me the tray just before she died and it has accompanied me on my travels all around the world.

Conclusion: why it is important —Whenever I use it, because it is meant to be used, I think about Katya and the wonderful hours we used to spend together.

READING | Lost property

Here are two letters which have been jumbled up. One is an informal letter to a friend; the other is more formal and is to a hotel.

1 Try to re-construct the letters by studying the opening and closing sentences for each letter and choosing from sentences **a** – **s** below.

> *Dear Sue,*
> *Just a note to say thank you for a lovely weekend at Pear Tree Cottage.*

> Dear Sir,
>   I am writing to say how much I enjoyed my weekend stay at your hotel.

> *Lots of love,*
> *May*

> Yours faithfully,
> *Julian January*
> (Julian January)

a I have searched for it but am unable to find it anywhere.
b Or else it could be near the tree where we had the picnic.
c Can't wait to see you at the conference on the 25th!
d You know, it's one of that pair of Victorian silver ones that father gave me for my birthday.
e I look forward to staying with you again on the weekend of the 25th.
f I had a really lovely time and the food was marvellous.
g If you find it, can you pop it in an envelope and send it to me?
h My wife would be most upset if it has been lost since it was a wedding present from her.
i You made me most welcome and the food was excellent.
j I've looked all over and I just can't find it.
k Not only is it valuable, but it is of great sentimental value.
l We must find it otherwise he'll start asking questions.
m I would appreciate it if you could check down the side of the sofas in the lounge.
n Failing that, it may be in room 307, where I stayed.
o Have a good look in the bathroom. That's where I probably dropped it.
p However, I believe I may have mislaid my cigarette case somewhere in the hotel.
q Should you discover it, I would be extremely grateful if you could send it to me.
r It is gold with the initials 'JJ' engraved on it.
s By the way, I think I left an earring at your place.

2 Make a list of the informal words and expressions which May uses in her letter. Can you think what their formal equivalents could be?

3 Writing

You recently spent the weekend with friends. However, you think you left something at their home. Write a letter thanking them for the weekend and asking about the lost object.

Gods in White Coats

A monster or a saint?

1 Quickly read the text and find out why Dr Kevorkian – the man in the picture – is in the news.

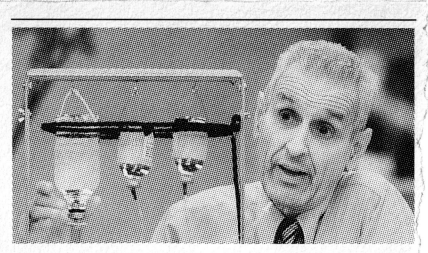

IN THE USA, a doctor is facing trial for helping a woman kill herself. Mrs Atkins, aged 54, contacted Dr Jack Kevorkian and explained that she wanted to end her life because she was suffering from an incurable disease. The doctor put his suicide machine into a van and he drove to a park where he told Mrs Atkins how to administer the fatal injection. If the court decides he killed Mrs Atkins, he could be jailed for life. In his defence, the doctor said: 'She knew what she was doing, she wanted to end her life. I asked her if she knew what that meant. She said, "Yes, I'm going to die. There's nothing for me. There's no life".' The police have taken the machine but Dr Kevorkian will help other people to end their lives unless he is kept in prison. In the doctor's own words he says: 'If they send me to jail, they'd better keep me there, otherwise I'll do it again when I get out.'

sity said: "Environmental issues have ... ly studying the effe...

2 Discussion points
1 Is Dr Kevorkian a saint or a monster?
2 What 'rights' should a person have over medical treatment? Should they be allowed to choose whether or not to die?
3 What do you think a court in your country would decide in Dr Kevorkian's case?
4 Since this story happened, a cure has been found for Mrs Atkins' disease. Does this change your opinion at all?

LANGUAGE STUDY

If, unless and otherwise

1 **Unless** can often be used to mean **if ... not**.

ACTION   RESULT

Unless you eat more fruit, your teeth will fall out!
If you don't eat more fruit, your teeth will fall out!

1 You won't get better if you don't rest. (**Unless**)
2 Unless they get here soon, they'll miss the train. (**If**)
3 If he doesn't eat less he'll get very fat. (**Unless**)
4 I'll report you unless you apologize. (**If**)
5 She won't be a dentist if she doesn't pass her exams. (**Unless**)

2 We can also express the same thing by using **had better** and **otherwise** at the beginning of the result clause.

*You'd better eat more fruit, **otherwise** your teeth will fall out!*

Re-write sentences 1–5 using **otherwise**.

WRITING PREPARATION

A letter of complaint

1 Put the paragraphs of this letter in the right order.

1
Yours sincerely,
Peter King

5
Fortunately, as it turned out, my sister was not badly injured, but the whole experience makes me very worried about more serious cases.

2
Let me give you an example of what I mean. Recently, my elder sister had a bad fall, and could not move, so I called an ambulance.

6
I am writing to you as our local spokesman to complain about our local hospital and the service it provides.

3
When it opened, it was clean and efficient and the wards well-staffed, but now, just a few years later, it appears to be badly organized and understaffed.

7
It was two hours before the ambulance arrived, and when my sister reached the hospital, she had to wait a further hour before she received attention from a nurse.

4
I realize that money and resources are limited, but I do urge you as our spokesman, to make clear publicly what the consequences could be for patients if the hospital services do not improve soon.

8
Dear Mr Greenaway,

2 How did you know which order to put them in?

45

SPEAKING

Food!

- What relationship does each person have with food?
- What will happen to the man on the left if he eats any more?
- If you were the brother or sister of the girl, how would you try to help her?

LISTENING

Discussing a problem

Frank is talking to Angie, a student who is helping out at the local youth club.

1 Listen for answers to these questions.

1 What is Frank's problem?
2 Does Angie really understand Frank's problem?

2 Listen again and fill in the gaps.

FRANK: I'm so ....[1]. It's ....[2].

ANGIE: So that's it. I thought you looked a bit ....[3].

FRANK: And the more I worry about it the more I seem to eat.

ANGIE: Frank, ...[4], what have you had to eat today?

FRANK: Well I didn't have breakfast so I ate a ....[5] on the way to school. Then I had a ....[6] at breaktime.

ANGIE: And what about at lunch?

FRANK: Um...a ....[7] and a cola.

ANGIE: It's no surprise you're getting fat. ....[8] is a balanced diet.

FRANK: What ....[9]?

ANGIE: Obviously, you're taking in too many calories. You ....[10] chocolate completely for a time and ....[11] all the snacks you eat. Also, ...[12] of those slimming clubs? You get advice on nutrition and they weigh you each week. It really works.

FRANK: How ....[13] about it?

3 Giving advice

What expressions does Angie use to give advice?

STUDENT A   turn to p. 137.   STUDENT B   turn to p. 141.

READING | Just puppy fat?

Here are three letters to a teenage magazine, but only two replies. Match up the two letters with their replies.

Dear Sally...

A
■ I'm really overweight and I hate dieting but I find the best way to lose weight is by going on a crash diet. The only problem is that I put the weight back on really quickly afterwards. What should I do?

B
■ I adore junk food like chips and hamburgers. My dad says it's really bad for me. Even so, I have never felt ill and have got a good figure. Should I take any notice of him?

C
One reason why you're not losing weight may simply be that you don't need to lose any. Another reason is you have probably got a bit of puppy fat. But whatever the reason, you should check with your doctor. If you are really overweight, you may have to go on a diet or take up some form of exercise. Your doctor will be able to advise you best.

D
My main advice is that you should give up these crash diets straight away. Trying to lose weight like this is dangerous. You should never miss main meals or allow yourself to feel too hungry. If you starve yourself, you'll pass out, or even worse! So look after your body. Go to a slimming club for some sensible nutritional advice.

E
■ Please can you help me? I'm really fed up. With every diet I've tried, I just can't seem to lose more than a couple of pounds. Even though I follow a diet carefully and never cheat, nothing seems to work.

WRITING | A letter of advice

Make a list of all the words and expressions which are used for requesting and giving advice. Write an answer to the third letter.

VOCABULARY | Phrasal verbs and health

Choose the correct phrasal verb to complete each sentence.

1 **A** *Look out* **B** *Look into* **C** *Look after* your teeth by brushing them regularly.
2 What a bad cough! If I were you I'd **A** *give out* **B** *give away* **C** *give up* smoking.
3 You'd better **A** *cut off* **B** *cut down* **C** *cut out* on the amount of coffee you drink.
4 To stay healthy, people ought to **A** *take out* **B** *take in* **C** *take up* exercise.
5 Has Mrs Brown **A** *got on with* **B** *got over* **C** *got away with* her operation.
6 I feel faint; I think I'm going to **A** *pass up* **B** *pass away* **C** *pass out*.

READING

It's all in the eye

1 Read the text quickly and find out the connection between an owl and medicine.

Iridology is the study of the eye's iris, used to diagnose someone's state of health and warn patients of potential problems. The underlying theory is that the entire body is reflected in the iris.

Iridology is for diagnosis only and not for treatment. However, many iridologists are practising homeopaths, herbalists or acupuncturists. The study of the iris not only indicates current health, but identifies potential weaknesses, many of which we inherit from our parents. By identifying a condition before it becomes a problem, people can minimize it or avoid it through changes to diet and lifestyle.

Iridology has a long history. It was practised in Ancient Egypt, and Hippocrates mentions it, too. The Hungarian, Dr Ignatz von Peczely (1822-1911) is the founder of iridology as a modern science. When he was a boy, he accidently broke the leg of his pet owl and noticed a dark mark appear in the bird's eye. As the leg healed, the mark disappeared. When von Peczely became a doctor, he developed a map showing the relationship of different parts of the body to the iris.

Iridology works because the iris records everything that has happened to the body since the age of six. It also carries genetic information which indicates future problems. The colour of the iris also provides the practitioner with vital information.

2 Choose the best option from the alternatives **A** and **B**.

1 Iridology is
 A a form of treatment.
 B a way of identifying a health problem.
2 Ignatz von Peczely
 A was the first person to notice iris markings.
 B re-established iridology.
3 What did von Peczely notice about the injured bird?
 A A new mark in the owl's eye.
 B The mark disappeared before the leg healed.
4 Iridology
 A can provide an early health warning.
 B is a form of fortune telling.

LISTENING

1 Key vocabulary
Study the simplified iridology diagram of the eye's iris. Can you unjumble the italic letters to find the names of four parts of the body?

2 Listen and answer these questions.

1 Why did Paola become an iridologist?
2 According to Paola what problems are people with
 a blue eyes likely to suffer from?
 b brown eyes likely to suffer from?
3 What is the reason for
 a hazel-coloured eyes?
 b green eyes?
4 What does Paola say about
 a Annie's general health?
 b her medical history?

LANGUAGE STUDY
The present perfect and past simple

1 Some time in the past

Paola says: *I **have been** a pharmacist.
I **trained** as one and **practised** for a few years.*

When we talk about our general experiences, we use the PRESENT PERFECT.
If we go on to give more detail, or give a specific time, then we use the PAST SIMPLE. In other words, we move from the indefinite past to the definite past.

Paola also says: *I **have** never **taken** a sleeping pill in my life.* (= in her life up to now.)

Read the short paragraph about Dr Frederick Wilberforce and put the verbs in *italics* into the appropriate form. (Dr Wilberforce is still working.)

Dr. Frederick Wilberforce is now a famous doctor but in his lifetime he (1) .... (*be*) a soldier and an explorer and (2) .... (*live*) in many different countries. When he (3) .... (*leave*) the army, he (4) .... (*study*) medicine and then (5) .... (*work*) in Africa. His first wife (6) .... (*be*) a doctor too, but she (7) .... (*die*) of malaria. Dr. Wilberforce (8) .... (*have*) a long and interesting career. Over the years, he (9) .... (*save*) thousands of lives and (10) .... (*perform*) hundreds of operations. The medical profession (11) .... (*give*) him many prizes; he (12) ....(*win*) the first for the work he did in the Third World. In addition, he (13) .... (*write*) several books on surgery. He (14) .... (*publish*) his latest one last year. He (15) .... (*not become*) very rich, like many other surgeons, because he (16) .... (*never believe*) in private medicine. Instead, he (17) .... (*always work*) in state hospitals.

2 The unfinished past

Look at these other sentences from the listening.

PAOLA: *There's something wrong with your left knee though. I can see that **you have hurt it at some time**.* (indefinite past)

ANNIE: *I had quite a bad skiing accident two years ago. I had an operation, but **it has bothered me ever since**.* (unfinished past)

Decide whether the verb in the following sentences expresses the idea of the indefinite or the unfinished past.

1 He has smoked since he was eighteen.
2 Johnny has broken his leg three times.
3 He has worked in a London hospital since he returned to England.
4 He has travelled widely in Africa.
5 They have lived here for many years.

3 Talking about an activity

When we are talking about an activity which started in the past and is still going on, we may use the PRESENT PERFECT CONTINUOUS.

ANNIE: *How long have you been an iridologist?*
PAOLA: *I've been practising for about seven years now.*

How would Paola have answered if she had used **since** instead of **for**?

4 Complete the second sentence so that it means the same as the one above it.

1 He passed his dentist's exams ten years ago.
   He has ....
2 They have been dieting for three months.
   They started ....
3 When did you start to train as a doctor?
   How long have ....?
4 She fell asleep when the doctor left.
   She has ....
5 The children's ward has been open for nine months.
   The children's ward ....

SPEAKING

Guinea pigs

In some clinics in London, people can agree to be 'guinea pigs' for medical experiments; they stay in hospitals like luxury hotels and earn a lot of money if they are prepared to take the medicines the doctors give them. In one place which experiments with new medical equipment, they pay people £10,000 if they agree to have toes cut off then sewn back on again!

- Would you agree to do this?
- How much money would you want for the 'toe experiment'?
- In some countries, prisoners serving long sentences can get out of prison sooner if they agree to take part in medical experiments. What do you think of this?

WRITING

Reading and summarizing

1 Six people are expecting operations today. However, for technical reasons, only one operating theatre is available and there is a maximum of eight hours' operating time. The patients who are not operated on today may have to wait another month. Read the details about the patients and make notes in the chart opposite.

Richard Bloom.
Aged 43. An ex-soldier who won medals for bravery. He has been a tramp since leaving the army seven years ago. He needs a kidney transplant almost immediately, and following a car accident, donor kidneys are available. *Operation time - 3 hours.*

Professor Muriel Greene.
Aged 74. She has been waiting for a replacement hip operation for three years. She is in great pain and her quality of life is poor. Her daughter has had to give up her job to look after her. Her operation has been cancelled twice already. *Operation time - 2 hours.*

Carlos Rodriguez.
Aged 32. He is a political refugee and a famous guitar player in his own country. He fell and broke his hand and needs immediate surgery if he is to continue playing. One day he could go back to take up an important position in government. *Operation time - 1 hour.*

Pauline Bolton.
Aged 36. A housewife and mother of five young children. Six months ago, her face was badly burned in an accident and she needs plastic surgery. She is extremely depressed about her appearance. *Operation time - 3 hours.*

Lorna Dobson.
Aged 17. Lorna has had a serious heart problem since she was born. She is getting weaker and will probably only live another year without an operation. Her family could afford private surgery, but her aunt, a politician, is against private health care. *Operation time - 5 hours.*

Arthur Griffiths.
Aged 57. Married with two grown-up children. An important and devoted trade union official. He has a serious lung disease caused by his time as a miner. His long-term prospects are poor, but an immediate operation to remove a diseased lung could give him two more years of active life. *Operation time - 2 hours.*

NAMES	FOR	AGAINST
Lorna Dobson	*Needs operation now. / Young.*	*Why can't family pay? Long operation*
Richard Bloom		
Carlos Rodriguez		
Prof. Greene		
Pauline Bolton		
Arthur Griffiths		

2 When you have finished, compare your chart with a partner.

3 These two paragraphs give possible answers. Which paragraph:
- almost repeats the language of the original texts.
- explains more successfully *why* the people should be chosen.
- is more logical.
- looks at the situation in more detail.

1 I would give operations to Lorna Dobson and Richard Bloom. Lorna is only 17 and will probably only live for a year without heart surgery. This operation takes five hours, so I would give Richard Bloom an operation in the remaining three hours. He is 43 and an ex-soldier. We have to look after our soldiers.
2 I would give operations to Lorna Dobson and Richard Bloom. Lorna needs the operation now as her condition is growing worse every day. She is the youngest patient and deserves a long and healthy life. Even though other patients have serious conditions, I think that Richard Bloom deserves his operation first. Society must show that it can look after its ex-soldiers, who have risked their lives for their country. His condition is weak but he could make a good recovery.

What is missing from both paragraphs?

4 Now write a short paragraph of your own saying who you think should have an operation today. Give reasons for your choices.

Genius

SPEAKING

Famous faces

Try to identify these famous people and say what they are or were famous for.

VOCABULARY

Professions

Very often we can form the profession by adding a suffix to the verb, for example, someone who teaches is **a teacher** (teach + **er**). Some professions are based on a verb or noun and end in **-or** (*man*)/**-ess** (*woman*), **-ist** or **-ian**, for example mathemati**cian**. Try to complete the following sentences.

Someone who…

1 is involved in politics is a ....
2 acts is an .... (*man*) .... (*woman*).
3 writes stories or novels is a ....
4 sings in opera is an ....
5 plays tennis is a ....
6 explores the world is an ....
7 comes up with new inventions is an ....
8 studies science is a ....
9 thinks about the meaning of life is a ....
10 paints or makes statues is an ....
11 composes music is a ....
12 plays a musical instrument is a ....
13 directs films is a ....

LANGUAGE STUDY

The past simple passive

1 Active to passive

*Shakespeare + **wrote** + Hamlet.* → *Hamlet **was written by** Shakespeare.*
SUBJECT + VERB + OBJECT   SUBJECT + to be + PAST + AGENT
*   PARTICIPLE*

2 Practice: quiz time

In teams, write ten questions about famous people. Take it in turns to ask and answer them. Where you can, use the simple past passive. There will be two points for each answer: one for the correct information and one for perfect English. (There are no points for the wrong information!)

SPEAKING

A party for all time

Imagine that you could hold a party for eight guests from today or history. Which eight people would you invite and why? You can ask ONE guest ONE very important or personal question only. Who would you ask, and what would your question be?

LISTENING

In an art gallery

1 Listen to the conversation between Jane and Phil.

1 Do they have the same taste in painting?
2 Which paintings does Jane like? Which paintings does Phil like?

2 Listen again and put these adjectives in the right order.
terrible   fascinating   gorgeous   awful   fantastic   marvellous

Which adjectives express the ideas of:
very good, *very bad*, *extremely beautiful* and *very interesting*?

3 Stress for emphasis
Listen again to these sentences from the conversation. Notice how Jane and Phil use stress and intonation to emphasize what they say.

I think it's fascinating.   All those gorgeous colours!

4 Practice
Work in pairs. Discuss the paintings. Say *why* you do or don't like them.

STUDENT A   you like painting 1; you hate 2 and 3.

STUDENT B   you adore paintings 2 and 3; you hate 1.

LANGUAGE STUDY

Reported speech

1 Look at these two sentences.

DIRECT SPEECH: *'It's awful, I don't like it at all.'*
REPORTED SPEECH: *Jane said (that) it was awful and (that) she didn't like it at all.*

2 Study the examples and then complete the information on tense changes.

DIRECT SPEECH	REPORTED SPEECH
1 "My memory **is** excellent."	She said her memory **was** excellent.
2 "I **passed** all my exams."	She told me she **had passed** all her exams.
3 "I **have worked** very hard."	She said she **had worked** very hard.
4 "**Will** I **win** a prize, Paul?"	She asked Paul if she **would win** a prize.
5 "What **would** you give me?"	She wanted to know what he **would** give her.

Tense changes: **present simple** → ....
.... → **past perfect**
present perfect → ....
.... → **would**

3 Finish each sentence so that it means the same as the one printed above it.

1 'True genius is very rare,' said the expert.
The expert said that ....
2 Frank told me he had bought a new computer.
Frank said,'..,'.
3 'Do you think I'll fail my driving test?' Sally asked.
Sally asked me ....
4 'Mozart wrote music at the age of four,' she said.
She said that ....
5 'Alice, I'm leaving soon,' said Tom.
Tom told ....
6 Mary asked, 'How much is the painting?'
Mary asked how ....

WRITING

A description of a painting

Which of the two paintings does the text describe? Make any changes you think necessary to describe the other painting.

One of my favourite paintings is Les Coquelicots *('poppies') by the Impressionist Claude Monet. It was painted in 1873 and is a charming scene of a stroll through a field full of poppies on a late summer's day. In the foreground we can see a woman and a small child, who seems to be dressed in a sailor's suit. Behind them, further along the way, they are being followed by another woman and child. In the background, there is a row of trees and a house under a cloudy sky. I think I like this picture so much because the artist has managed to capture the time of day and year and moment perfectly. Of course, it was not painted in great detail, like many of the classical paintings that went before; instead it is a delightful impression of a moment in time.*

SPEAKING

Work in pairs.

STUDENT A look at the picture on p. 138. **STUDENT B** look at the picture on p. 142.

Without showing each other your picture, take it in turns to describe it to your partner, who should try to draw it.

READING

A tragic genius

1 Before you read the biography of Vincent Van Gogh, tell each other what you know about him. He painted several self-portraits; this one was painted shortly before his death. What does it say about the artist?

2 Read the text and decide whether these statements are **true** or **false**.

1 He always had a difficult character.
2 He never married.
3 He lost his job as a missionary because he didn't take it seriously enough.
4 His earlier work was bright and colourful.
5 He never had any formal training.
6 He went to Japan to study its art.
7 His relatives forced him into the asylum.
8 He killed himself in Arles.
9 He never sold a painting.
10 All his work was produced in ten years.

Vincent Van Gogh was born in Holland in 1853. His father was a Protestant pastor. His boyhood was happy although he was a moody and solitary child. (1) .... he was sixteen he joined the art-dealing firm Goupil, where his uncle was a partner. Four years later he went to London where he had an unhappy love affair and lost his job. Vincent remained single.

(2) .... working as a teacher he became a missionary among poor coal miners. He gave away everything he owned and was dismissed (3) .... for taking Christ's teaching too literally. He lost his faith but in 1880 found his vocation as an artist. He worked (4) .... four busy years producing drawings and dark watercolours of peasant life. (5) .... now, he had been self taught, so he went to work with the landscape artist Anton Mauve. After a row he returned to his family. (6) .... his stay with them he produced his best early work: The Potato Eaters.

Vincent went to Paris where his brother Theo was working for Goupil's. There he was deeply influenced by the Impressionists and the simple but striking design of Japanese prints. This was the turning point of his career. (7) .... he progressed he developed his own style and used brighter colours to express his feelings.

In February 1888 he went to Arles in the south of France, searching for a brighter, 'Japanese' light. He rented a house which he painted yellow, and produced some cheerful pictures. He invited Gaugin to join him and (8) .... a long delay, he came, but they got on badly and Vincent threatened to kill his guest who left. To show he was sorry Vincent cut off his ear.

(9) .... terrified of madness, he entered the asylum of Saint-Remy de Provence. Despite periods of mental illness, he painted two hundred pictures, including much of his famous work. However, his mental condition worsened and he killed himself. Today, his paintings sell for millions – (10) .... his life he sold just one.

LANGUAGE STUDY

Time expressions

1 Study these example sentences and the diagrams which explain common time expressions.

A We always eat **before** 7 o'clock (not at 7 or after 7).

B I'll wait **until** 7 o'clock (but I'll leave at 7 on the dot).

C We must leave **by** 7 o'clock (before 7 or at 7, but no later).

D (i) I was at home **for** two hours earlier today (the period of time between 12 and 2).

(ii) I have been at home **for** two hours now, (the period of time between 5 and 7).

E I have been at home **since** 12.00. (It's now 7.)

I got home.
I am still at home.

F Please deliver the sofa sometime **during** the afternoon (any time between 12.00 and 5).

G g Study the following uses of **as**.

(i) **As** we left the museum, it started to rain.
We left the museum.
It started to rain.

(ii) **As** she grew older, she became more tolerant.

She grew older.
— 15 — 30 — 45 →
She became more tolerant.

2 Look back at the time expressions in Unit 1, Set E and Unit 2, Set C.

3 Now complete the text using each of the following time expressions. Use each one once only.

this time	after	for	until	when
during	as	by now	during	after

SPEAKING

- Many famous people seem to have tragic lives. If you had a choice, would you like a happy but unremarkable life or an exceptional but unhappy one?
Does a genius have to be mad or different in some way?

LISTENING

The sad geniuses

Children who are born autistic never really learn normal social skills. However, they sometimes have remarkable abilities, as the case of Ellen Boudreaux shows.

1 Listen to the description of Ellen Boudreaux and tick (√) her abilities.

1 She could hum a melody when she was still a baby. ☐
2 She was able to walk when she was just four months old. ☐
3 She can sense the position of objects. ☐
4 She can use radar equipment. ☐
5 She can sing any song she has ever heard. ☐
6 She can speak fluently on most topics. ☐
7 She is able to answer any questions of general knowledge she is asked. ☐
8 She has no idea of time. ☐

2 Did you find out anything which you thought was unusual or remarkable? Have you heard of any similar cases?

LANGUAGE STUDY

1 Listen again and list the different ways in which the speaker describes ability.

2 Tell each other at what age you were able to: walk, speak, tell the time, tie your shoelaces, dress yourself, ride a bicycle, swim, read and write.
Do you think you were 'advanced', 'average' or 'backward' for your age?

3 Expand these notes to tell us about the extraordinary abilities of Alonzo Clemons.

NOTES

- normal baby until age of three
- bad fall and brain damage
- poor speech
- very low intelligence
- aged 25, count to ten
- sculpts constantly
- only needs to see something once
- sculpts in the dark
- makes a horse in twenty minutes
- has sold over 500 pieces

4 Separable phrasal verbs 🔘

When an object comes between the verb and the particle, the particle is normally stressed more than the verb. Listen to these sentences and repeat them.

1 Turn it **off**.
2 Why don't you try them **on**?
3 I can't make it **out**.
4 Shall we take him **in**?
5 Could you turn it **down**?

6 If I were you, I'd give it **away**.
7 He made the story **up**.
8 When can you pay me **back**?
9 The operator cut us **off**.
10 The bad weather held us **up**.

WRITING

The life of Mozart

The composer Wolfgang Amadeus Mozart's life has all the ingredients of tragedy. Expand these notes to produce a short biography of Mozart. Refer to the work on time expressions and 'ability'.

NOTES

- born in 1756
- son of composer and violinist Leopold Mozart
- played harpsichord and composed at age of four
- 1762 – toured Germany and France
- incredible abilities – in Rome 1770, heard a complicated piece twice, wrote it down perfectly!
- continued to tour
- composer and performer
- no permanent position
- worked for Archbishop of Salzburg 1779–81
- unhappy period
- went to Vienna
- wrote much of greatest work: operas *Marriage of Figaro* 1786 and *Don Giovanni* 1787
- Italian composer Salieri great rival and jealous of Mozart
- Mozart poor and overworked
- died 1791, typhus (or poisoned by Salieri?)
- Mozart died in poverty
- wrote 49 symphonies, four famous operas and many concertos

SPEAKING Look at the photograph of the headmistress and pupils of a certain school. What kind of school is it? How do you think the pupils get on with their headmistress?

The last school to cane its girls

IN NEARLY ALL SCHOOLS IN ENGLAND, pupils who misbehave are just told off by the teacher. However, at the expensive Rodney School naughty girls are punished by caning. The headmistress, Miss Thomas, who has run the school for 47 years, says that she only canes the girls to shame them rather than hurt them.

Surprisingly, the girls back their headmistress up; if they have been up to no good, they believe that they deserve to be punished. One girl, Adele Kirkman, was given three strokes on each hand for going into the nearby town without her school uniform. To be fair, Adele was allowed to choose between writing a long essay, staying in the school grounds for three weeks, or the cane. She chose the cane because it was quicker. Another girl Nicola Whitely, then twelve, chose to be caned too, because she had been caught in her dormitory with some boys.

When she phoned her father, he told her, 'Think of all the things you have got away with. This time you have been caught.'

READING

1 Read the text and decide if your assumptions were correct.

2 Phrasal verbs in context
Find the four phrasal verbs in the text and match them with the following meanings: *to criticize, to be in the act of doing, to escape punishment for, to support.*

3 Discuss these questions in groups.

1 What do you think of the girls' attitude to punishment?
2 Which punishment would you have chosen if you'd been Adele?
3 What do you think of Nicola Whitely's father?
4 Do you think the girls will be good adults and parents?
5 What sort of punishment exists in schools in your country?
6 Have you ever been unfairly punished? If so, when?

4 Look at these 'crimes' some pupils commit. Which three are the most serious and which three are the least serious?

> ~~smoking~~　　　　　　　　　　　~~being rude to the teacher~~
>
> ~~being late without a good excuse~~　~~not doing homework~~
>
> ~~cheating in an examination~~　　　~~fighting~~
>
> ~~stealing~~　　　　　　　　　　　~~not wearing school uniform~~
>
> ~~playing truant~~　　　　　　　　~~bullying~~

LISTENING

Crime and punishment in the classroom

1 Write down Tim's descriptions of Angela and Mr Gilbert.
2 What do you think about Tim, Angela and Mr Gilbert?
3 What do you think happened next and what were the consequences for Tim?

LANGUAGE STUDY

Describing physical appearance

1 Study the tapescript of the listening text on page 153 and notice how **to have**, **to be** and **with** are used.

2 Imagine that you once knew the people in the photograph below. Use the same sentence patterns and the words in the box to write descriptions of them.

> eyelashes　wrinkles　scar　dark　curly　eyebrows　moustache　straight　fair

WRITING

'I shall never forget what happened…'

Like Tim, you have probably had a memorable or embarrassing experience. Perhaps it was associated with school.
Write a paragraph similar to the one you have heard describing:

- when and where it happened/how old you were.
- the people in the story and what they looked like.
- what happened and how you felt.
- what the consequences were (if there were any).

VOCABULARY
Education

1 Look at these names of educational institutions in England and use them to complete the definitions.

> polytechnic university college nursery school
> secondary school kindergarten primary school

1 Young children often attend a .... or a
.... , where they learn to get on with
other children, play educational games, etc.
2 Pupils attend a .... between the ages of
five and eleven.
3 Pupils attend a .... between the ages of
eleven and sixteen or eighteen. This is where they
take their GCSE and/or A level examinations.
4 Older students can attend a .... ,
.... or .... for higher
education and further qualifications (e.g. a degree).

Which educational institutions do you attend in your
country and at what ages do you attend them?

2 Match the names with the definitions.

> lecturer apprentice professor coach instructor

1 someone who trains a sports team
2 someone who teaches a skill like skiing or driving
3 someone who teaches at a university, college or
polytechnic
4 someone who works with an experienced person
for a number of years to learn a trade or skill
5 someone who heads a university department

Now read these extracts and decide who is speaking in
each case. How do you know?

▪ 'M.S.M. Mirror signal manoeuvre. I want you to
turn left at the traffic lights. Look in your mirror.
All clear?'
▪ 'Carefully now carefully. If in doubt measure it
again. Remember, if you cut a piece off you can't
put it back!'
▪ 'I'm very disappointed with your results. If you
don't do better when you take them again, you'll
have to leave. Degree courses are tough and we
can't lower our standards just for you.'
▪ 'Right, we may be a goal down but everything's
to play for. This half, take the game to them.'

READING
All I really need to know...

1 Look at the pictures of kindergarten life.
Can you identify what the children are doing?

2 Think about your own early years at school. Did
you learn any lessons that have helped you later on?
Find out from your partner(s) what they learned from
their first experience of school.

3 Read the text about the lessons the writer learned
at kindergarten in America.
Which lessons do you think are a) very important b)
quite important c) not necessary?

All I really need to know
about how to live and what
to do and how to be, I
learned in Kindergarten.
These are the things I learned:
Share everything.
Play fair.
Don't hit people.
Put things back where you found them.
Clean up your own mess.
Don't take things that aren't yours.
Say you're sorry when you hurt somebody.
Wash your hands before you eat.
Flush.
Warm cookies and cold milk are good for you.
Live a balanced life – learn some and draw
and paint and sing and dance and play and
work every day some.
Take a nap every afternoon.
When you go out into the world, watch out for
traffic, hold hands, and stick together.
Be aware of wonder. Remember the little seed
in the Styrofoam cup: the roots go down and
the plant goes up and nobody really knows
how or why, but we are all like that.
Goldfish and hamsters and white mice and
even the little seed in the Styrofoam cup –
they all die. So do we.
And then remember the *Dick and Jane* books
and the first word you learned – the biggest
word of all – LOOK.

SPEAKING

Lost lessons

Which lessons have these people forgotten?

1 Peter Jones never tidied his room. His mother had to do it.
2 Jenny Brown won the lottery but did not give her family any money.
3 Sam Smith ran across the road and was hit by a car.
4 Pat Fisher worked so hard that she lost all her friends.
5 Chris Lee always cheated at card games. In the end, no one would play with him.
6 A rich man had his body frozen so that future scientists could bring him back to life, but somebody turned the freezer off by mistake!

LANGUAGE STUDY

Indefinite pronouns

1 **Some-, any-, no-:**
*Say you're sorry when you hurt **somebody**.*

Study these sentences and answer the questions.

A I need **somebody/someone** to talk to, **something** to eat and **somewhere** to sleep.
B I haven't got **anybody/anyone** to talk to, **anything** to eat or **anywhere** to sleep.
C Is there **anybody/anyone** to talk to, **anything** to eat or **anywhere** to sleep?
D There's **nobody/no one** to talk to, **nothing** to eat and **nowhere** to sleep.

Which form (**some-, any-, no-**) do we use:

1 in questions?
2 in statements with a positive sense?
3 in statements with a negative sense but a positive structure?
4 in sentences with negative structures?

2 **Every-:** *Share **everything**.*
Replace the italic words with an indefinite pronoun beginning with **every-**.

1 We asked *all the people there.*
2 She ate *all there was to eat.*
3 I looked *all over the house* for the keys.

3 Complete the passage with an appropriate indefinite pronoun.

I had been sleeping when (1) .... woke me up. There was a funny noise coming from downstairs. I went to the top of the stairs and said, 'Is (2) .... there?' (3) .... answered! Feeling a little braver, I looked in the sitting room, in the cupboards and in the dining room. In fact I looked (4) .... Finally I went into the kitchen. I saw (5) .... standing by the fridge. I screamed and turned on the light. It was my flat mate, Julian. 'Sorry,' he said, 'I got up because I felt like (6) .... to eat so I had a few biscuits but I dropped the tin.' I looked in the tin, there was (7) .... there. He had eaten (8) ....

63

READING

Interpreting information

1 Compulsory education in Britain lasts until the age of 16, when pupils may leave school and start work.

Look at the end-of-year results of four pupils (**B**elinda **G**rey, **A**rnold **R**oberts, **R**atan **P**atel and **A**lison **D**ukes) and answer the questions.

1 Who is best at Mathematics?
2 What is Alison Dukes' best subject?
3 What is Ratan Patel's worst subject?
4 Is Arnold Roberts better at arts or science subjects?
5 In your opinion, who are the most 'practical' and who are the most 'academic'?

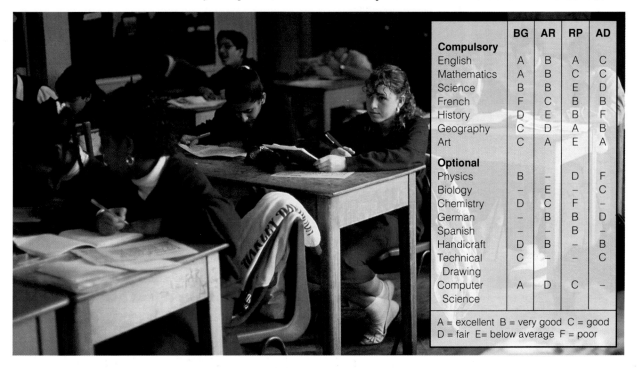

	BG	AR	RP	AD
Compulsory				
English	A	B	A	C
Mathematics	A	B	C	C
Science	B	B	E	D
French	F	C	B	B
History	D	E	B	F
Geography	C	D	A	B
Art	C	A	E	A
Optional				
Physics	B	–	D	F
Biology	–	E	–	C
Chemistry	D	C	F	–
German	–	B	B	D
Spanish	–	–	B	–
Handicraft	D	B	–	B
Technical Drawing	C	–	–	C
Computer Science	A	D	C	–

A = excellent B = very good C = good
D = fair E = below average F = poor

2 Write sentences comparing the performance of Ratan Patel and Alison Dukes at the compulsory subjects. Check the box for help.

	Comparatives	*Superlatives*
Short adjectives:	short**er than**	short**est**
Long adjectives:	**more** / **less** beautiful **than**	**the** **most** / **least** beautiful
Remember:	**Good** ... **better than** ... **the best** **Bad** ... **worse than** ... **the worst**	
	as *adjective* **as** (= *the same*)	

Example: *Alison Dukes is bad at Science but Ratan is even worse.*

3 Compare the performance of all four pupils at French, History and Science.

LANGUAGE STUDY

Adjective + preposition

*Ratan Patel is **good at** languages.*

1 Match the adjectives with prepositions.

1	good/bad	**A**	in
2	keen	**B**	of
3	interested	**C**	with
4	tired	**D**	at
5	disappointed	**E**	on

2 Look at the pupils' results again and complete these sentences with the most appropriate combination of adjective and preposition. In some cases, you will have to use the superlative form of the adjective.

1 Belinda Grey seems to be very .... French.
2 Ratan Patel must be quite .... languages; after all, he got two Bs.
3 Alison Dukes was probably .... her results in History and Physics.
4 Ratan Patel probably isn't .... Science; if he liked it more, he would probably do better.
5 Belinda is the .... Maths and Alison is the .... Physics.
6 However, Belinda finds languages boring. If she were more .... them, she would do much better.
7 Arnold Roberts is .... Biology; he has been studying it too long!

SPEAKING

Role play

Parents, teachers and pupils are meeting to discuss the futures of the four pupils. Form groups of three. Your teacher will give you each a role – parent, teacher or pupil. Read the notes on the particular pupil and then act out the meeting.

Ratan Patel
Wants to leave school but his parents want him to stay until he is eighteen. Ratan's ambition – to be a travel agent. Will need A levels for this.

Belinda Grey
Father a successful businessman. Disappointed with his daughter's performance. Belinda wants to study electronic engineering at university but does not have much self-confidence.

Arnold Roberts
Parents both dentists. Want Arnold to become a dentist and join their practice. Arnold is worried about disappointing his parents. But would he make a good dentist?

Alison Dukes
Parents both want her to stay at school until she is eighteen. She is tired of school, wants to leave. Has been offered an apprenticeship in the fashion business. Would like to accept it.

LISTENING

A miraculous way to learn?

Kay Able is talking to Dr Brian Green, a lecturer in psychology, about a new approach to language learning. The interview is in three short parts.

1 **Part A** Listen to the first part of the interview and label the diagram to show which functions belong to which half of the brain.

2 **Part B** Listen for the answers to these questions.

1 Which side of the brain do most teaching methods use?
2 What is the problem with this?
3 Why does Dr Green mention songs and rhymes? Does the interviewer agree?

3 **Part C** Listen, and tick the special features of the method Dr Green describes.

1 It involves singing. ☐
2 Students have to meditate. ☐
3 The teacher speaks in an unnatural way. ☐
4 Students try to draw the words on paper. ☐
5 The students listen to music while they study. ☐

- Does this seem a good way of learning to you?
- How do you remember new words?

LANGUAGE STUDY

Revision of adverbs

1 Complete the second sentence with an adverb so that it means the same as the first.

1 He is a bad player.   – He plays ....
2 He is a slow learner.   – He learns ....
3 He was a hard worker.   – He worked ....
4 She has got a beautiful voice. – She sings ....
5 He is a fast walker.   – He walks ....
6 She is a quick thinker.   – She thinks ....
7 She is a good writer.   – She writes ....

2 Important differences

Study the three pairs of sentences. Note the difference between the words in **bold**.

1a She is studying **hard**. **1b** She is **hardly** studying.
2a She never comes **late** to school. **2b** She hasn't been to school **lately**.
3a Exam time is getting **near**. **3b** She **nearly** failed her exams.

3 Which of these comments could you add to which sentence above?

a Perhaps she's sick. **d** She's always on time.
b What a lazy girl! **e** She had a lucky escape.
c Just another two weeks! **f** She does two hours' homework every morning.

4 Which words in **bold** mean: *not on time, not much, close, almost, recently, a lot*?

WRITING | Learning to swim

1 What is going on in the picture? How do you think the child feels?
Do you remember learning to swim? How did you feel?

2 Quickly read through the text and find out the different stages the writer went through when she was learning how to swim.

● What did you think of the teacher's method?
● Could it be applied to other kinds of learning?

3 Punctuate the text and arrange it into three paragraphs.

i shall never forget how i learned to swim i was nine years old and like many other children i was terrified of the water however my teacher miss townsend had a wonderful system for teaching swimming it worked with nine children out of ten once a week we all went to the swimming pool the first couple of times we got used to the water and splashed about in the shallow end after that we had a kind of board which helped us to float when we moved up and down the pool by kicking our legs by now most us knew how to float but we did not have the confidence to swim on our own our teacher had a brilliant idea she took two ordinary cotton reels and tied a long piece of string between them i held one of them and miss townsend held the other and i swam for the very first time supported by my belief in the power of the tiny cotton reel

4 Now write a story about how you were taught to do something.

UNIT 8 | *City Life*

SPEAKING

Look at these photographs.
Which cities do you associate with them?

LISTENING

City thoughts

Listen to the thoughts of people in some of the photographs. Who do the thoughts belong to? How do you know?

VOCABULARY

1 Choose the most appropriate word to complete each sentence.

1 When I went to Paris, I was impressed by its .... transport service.
A civil **B** private **C** public

2 Instead of blocking London's busy streets, travellers should use the ....
A coach **B** metro **C** underground

3 In New York, the underground railway is known as the ....
A motorway **B** subway **C** tram

4 Passengers always complain when train .... go up.
A fees **B** fares **C** prices

5 In some countries, people move to big cities because they think they will have a better .... of living.
A level **B** standard **C** cost

6 The city's atmosphere has been so .... by car exhaust fumes that you can hardly breathe.
A stained **B** polluted **C** gassed

7 This problem is made worse by the terrible traffic .... which block the main roads.
A lights **B** crowds **C** jams

8 .... is one of London's most important industries.
A Sightseeing **B** Tourism **C** Visiting

9 Most big cities suffer from .... problems.
A social **B** sociable **C** society

10 You often see .... people sleeping in parks or begging.
A drug-addict **B** homeless **C** tramps

11 Why don't you rent a room in a .... if you haven't got much money?
A hotel **B** landlady **C** hostel

12 Millions of London's workers have long train journeys from the ....
A outside **B** suburban **C** suburbs

13 Such people are known as ....
A computers **B** trainers **C** commuters

14 In the .... hour, they may have to stand up all the way.
A traffic **B** busy **C** rush

15 It often .... them hours to get home.
A needs **B** takes **C** wants

16 However, they feel it is worth the .... to live outside the city.
A voyage **B** trip **C** journey

SPEAKING

1 Try to describe the scenes in the photographs using as much of the vocabulary as you can from the previous exercise.

2 How do you think the people feel in each of the situations you can see?

WRITING

Poppy is a Greek student who is going to do an intensive English course in London. She has received a letter from a friend of her father's, who has arranged her accommodation for her.

1 Read the letter and put the paragraphs in the right order.

2 Look at the underground map on p. 75 and follow the route suggested by Martin.

1 Dear Poppy

2 Turn left just as you come out of the station and go straight on. Brooksville Avenue is the fifth road on the left. It's a ten-minute walk. If you've got a lot of luggage, then you could always get off the Underground at Hyde Park Corner and take a taxi.

3 She is an extremely nice woman in her fifties and has been a family friend for years. Her husband died two years ago so she lives alone. I have arranged for you to have bed and breakfast there, which will cost you £55 a week. You'll also be able to have limited use of the kitchen for basic cooking.

4 I am writing to confirm the arrangements for your accommodation while you are in London. Your father told me that you'll be arriving at Heathrow Airport on 20th September. I'll do my best to make sure someone from my office is there to meet you.

5 As I said, I am 99% certain you'll be met but, in case something goes wrong, this is how you get there. The best way of getting to the centre of London from Heathrow is by Underground. Take the Underground to Piccadilly Circus then change to a northbound Bakerloo train and get off at Queen's Park station. This part of the journey will take about fifty minutes.

6 All the same, I'd better give you the full name and address of your landlady just in case there are any problems:
Mrs Angela Hallam
98 Brooksville Lane
London NW13
Tel: 081-623-8990

7 I look forward to seeing you soon.
Best wishes,
Martin Smith

3 Question making

Poppy is phoning an American friend who wants to visit her in London.
What are her friend's questions?

1 ....?
  She's in her fifties.
2 ....?
  She was, but now she's a widow.
3 ....?
  £55 a week.
4 ....?
  Just light meals.
5 ....?
  Heathrow.
6 ....?
  No, you have to change at Piccadilly Circus.
7 ....?
  About fifty minutes.
8 ....?
  About a kilometre.
9 ....?
  No, the fifth.

4 Imagine someone is coming to visit you from abroad. Write a letter explaining how to reach you by public transport.

LISTENING

Two cities

Poppy has arrived at Mrs Hallam's in London.
Listen to their conversation. **Part A** is about London and **Part B** is about Athens.

1 **Part A** Listen once and answer these general questions.

1 How does Mrs Hallam feel about London?
2 How does Poppy react to what she hears?
3 What sort of person is Mrs Hallam?

2 **Part A** Listen again and find answers to these more specific questions.

1 When was Mrs Hallam's house built?
2 Why is London so spread out?
3 Why have people left the city for the countryside?
4 What does Mrs Hallam say about her own area?
5 What social problems does she mention?
6 Why did she move back to London?

3 **Part B** Listen once and answer these general questions.

1 Has Mrs Hallam ever been to Athens?
2 What big problem does Poppy mention?

4 **Part B** Listen once again. What solution has been tried?

WRITING

Summary writing

You are going to write a summary of the advantages and disadvantages of London and Athens.

1 Complete the grid with the main points from the conversation between Mrs Hallam and Poppy.

CITY	ADVANTAGES	DISADVANTAGES
London		
Athens		

2 Compare your grid with a partner and decide on the major points you will mention in your summary.

3 In your own words, write a paragraph summarizing the advantages and disadvantages of the two cities.

READING

Rome the transformer

1 In the 1970s, Denise Lawrence spent four years in Rome.

Quickly read the text and answer these key questions.

1 What was Denise like before she lived in Rome?
2 What effect did living in Rome have on her?
3 What's Denise's theory about becoming a Roman. What do you think of it?

2 Decide if these statements are true or false.

1 Southern Europe has helped to civilize the north.
2 Denise used to carefully control all aspects of her behaviour.
3 It is easy to become a Roman.
4 Denise believes it can be good to disobey rules.
5 It can be very dangerous to have a discussion in Rome.
6 The best way of crossing the road in Rome is to run.

The years I spent in Rome changed me. The city and its people civilized me. This is hardly surprising because Mediterranean cultures have been doing this to barbarians for centuries. It helps to explain the affection and gratitude the English feel for Italy, a country which has taught many of us how to live, feel and 'be'.

Before I lived in Rome, I was happy to own two scruffy pairs of jeans. I always waited for the green man at pedestrian crossings. I ate in order to exist. I queued obsessively (the *true* national sport in England) and never sounded the horn of a car in warning or frustration. I had probably never *really* enjoyed myself or lost my inhibitions.

Yet within a year of living in Rome, I was proud of my smart clothes, could fight my way onto a bus and play 'La Cucaracha' on my car horn from absolute joy. I no longer felt like a stranger — I felt I belonged there. I'm convinced that this could happen to anyone. Nor is there anything genetic about it: I've seen repressed English people and retiring Swedes and Germans totally adopt the behaviour of their hosts. If you went to live in Rome, you'd become a Roman, too.

Pretty quickly, you'd take more care of how you looked. You'd drink your coffee strong and black — not long and milky. You'd learn a healthy disrespect for petty rules and regulations. You'd develop the skills of a Grand Prix racing driver - and

be able to squeeze your car into a space with no room left for even a packet of cigarettes. You'd no longer walk past famous buildings with your mouth open like a Venus fly-trap – you'd take the Trevi Fountain and the Colosseum and Forum for granted. You'd be incapable of speech without moving your hands, yet be able to argue passionately without a hint of physical violence. You'd find pleasure in perfect food and drink and evenings spent in atmospheric cafés overlooking delightful squares.

However, the real test is this: while deep in conversation, step into the road and stroll casually across six lanes of speeding traffic confident that the cars will miss you. If you can do this, then you'll be a Roman.

LANGUAGE STUDY

The first and second conditional

1 Look at these two sentences.

a *If you move to Rome, you'll become a Roman too.*
b *If you moved to Rome, you'd become a Roman too.*

In which sentence does the speaker believe you may possibly move to Rome?
In which one does the speaker believe that this is unlikely (or even impossible)?

2 Whether we use the first or second conditional often depends on how likely we think something is. We often use the second conditional when we are imagining or day-dreaming:
If I had £1,000,000, I would buy a yacht. (But I'm quite ordinary; I'll never have £1,000,000.)

3 Study the 'probability meter' and the example, then expand the other words to make complete sentences using either the first or second conditional.

 SPEAKING

Cultural exchanges

Denise says she learnt a lot from living in Rome. What lessons could people from your country teach or learn from other cultures? Think about:

- driving
- working hard
- honesty
- enjoying food and drink
- music and fashion
- personal relationships

 WRITING

Just like you!

A foreigner really wants to become exactly like someone from your country. Write down the advice you would give.

Example

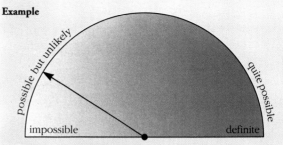

If/fewer tourists/go to Rome/it be less crowded.
If fewer tourists went to Rome it would be less crowded.

1 If I/eat less pasta/I/lose a lot of weight.

2 If Rome/less polluted/life/be much more pleasant.

3 If you/cross road now/you/get run over.

4 If you/cross road now/you/get run over.

5 If underground/be/more efficient/I/use it more often.

6 If you/enjoy/ice cream/you/be/in heaven in Rome.

7 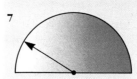 What/you do/if/I give you a plane ticket?

READING | London then and now

1 In this text about London, three sentences have been wrongly placed. Identify them and decide where you would put them.

2 Match the pictures with the pieces of text to which they refer.

London is on the River Thames about 40 miles from the coast. It has around 7,000,000 inhabitants. It was once the world's greatest port but nowadays it is a financial and tourist centre. Visitors who want a break from shopping can relax in its beautiful parks.

Perhaps it is most famous as the home of the British monarchy. Visitors can witness the timeless traditions surrounding it. However, the city has not seen only royalty and glamour . . .

In 1348, the Black Death killed half its population. In 1666, the Great Fire destroyed nearly all the old city. Since Edward the Confessor, Britain has had 47 rulers. During the war, bombs destroyed the docklands. Since then, they have been re-built as smart residential areas.

Today, the capital has something for everyone. It has some of the world's best department stores. Its cultural life is rich and varied; during the day, you can visit its museums which contain priceless treasures. In the evening its theatres offer a marvellous range of live entertainment. In 1665, it struck again and killed over a 1,000 a week.

With so much on offer, we have to agree with Dr Johnson's words: 'When a man is tired of London he is tired of life'.

WRITING

Answer these questions about London. Then use the same questions to make notes about your own town or capital city, and write about it.

1 Where is it and what is its population?
2 What are its origins and what is it known for today?
3 What are its history and traditions (good and bad things)?
4 What can visitors do?

LISTENING

Finding the way

LRT Registered user No. 92/1672

1 Poppy needs help to find a restaurant in Covent Garden. Listen and fill in the gaps in the dialogue.

POPPY: I was ....[1] help me, Mrs Hallam. I want to get to Covent Garden.

MRS HALLAM: Oh, yes. That's easy. Let's look at the Underground map. Right, we're in West London, so you ....[2] – that's the Bakerloo line – to Piccadilly Circus. Then ....[3] to the Piccadilly line, and ....[4] eastbound tube to Covent Garden.

POPPY: Thank you. How ....[5]?

MRS HALLAM: About half an hour.

Poppy is at Covent Garden but can't find the restaurant.

POPPY: Excuse me ....[6] tell me ....[7] Garrick Street?

PASSER-BY 1: Sorry, ...[8].

POPPY: Oh dear. Excuse me. ....[9] Garrick Street is?

PASSER-BY 2: Yes, but you're walking the wrong way. ....[10] the tube station, ...[11] fourth turning ....[12] and cut through into Garrick Street. It's only a couple of minutes' walk.

POPPY: Thanks a lot. ....[13] time, please?

PASSER-BY 2: Yes, it's 8.15.

2 Look at the completed texts and study the ways in which Poppy makes requests. How do Mrs Hallam and Passer-by 2 give Poppy directions?

SPEAKING

Giving directions

In pairs, using the Underground map ask for and give each other directions from:

- Notting Hill Gate to Charing Cross.
- The Elephant and Castle to Euston.
- Knightsbridge to Covent Garden.
- Piccadilly Circus to High Street Kensington.

As Others See Us

READING

A case of prejudice?

1 Before you read the article, study these dictionary definitions.

prejudice – (an example of) unfair and often unfavourable feeling or opinion not based on reason or enough knowledge: *a new law to discourage racial prejudice* (prejudice against members of other races); *a prejudice against women drivers*.

discrimination – -nated, -nating
1 (between) to see or make a difference (between two or more things or people): *you must try to discriminate between facts and opinions.* 2 (against/in favour of) usu. derog. to treat (a person or group) as worse/better than others: *This law discriminates against lower paid workers.*

2 Read the article and find out:
● who Nigel Benn is.
● what happened to him on the motorway.
● why the police apologized to Benn last year.

STOPPED BECAUSE I WAS A BLACK IN A WHITE PORSCHE

BOXING CHAMP NIGEL BENN claimed last night he was stopped by cops because he was a BLACK man driving a flashy WHITE sports car.

Benn, nicknamed 'the Dark Destroyer', said one officer alleged his £140, 000 Porsche 911 Turbo was stolen.

The twenty-six-year-old world middleweight champ said: 'The policeman tried to humiliate me because I was a black man driving an expensive car.'

It happened as Benn and his black manager, Ambrose Mendy, were driving in the slow moving traffic on the M25. The boxer was changing lanes when a policeman jumped out from a parked patrol car.

Benn said: 'He hit the roof of my car and said, "I believe this car is stolen." He was going crazy and kept swearing.'

'I said I was Nigel Benn, but he still gave me a ticket.'

Thames Valley Police said: 'Any complaint will be investigated.' Last January, police apologized to Benn after his picture was used as a 'wanted' photo in a hunt for a lookalike gunman.

3 Discussion

In pairs or groups, discuss these questions.

1 How far do you agree with the headline?
2 Do you think the police had a good reason for stopping Benn?
3 Do you agree that this is an example of racial prejudice?
4 What would have happened in your country?
5 In your experience, which groups are often the victims of prejudice?

VOCABULARY

Expressions associated with colours

Fill each gap with the name of a common colour to make idioms.

1 His arrival took everybody by surprise; it was completely **out of the** ....
2 She made me so angry, **I saw** ....
3 When he saw his neighbour's new car, he was .... **with envy**.
4 Draw your gun, sheriff! Or **are you too** .... ?
5 People in songs say they **feel** .... when they're unhappy.
6 The political situation **looks** .... I think there's going to be war.
7 Why do you always **see things in** .... **and** .... ? Life isn't like that; most things are grey.
8 She is **so** .... ; she'll believe anything anyone tells her.
9 It's better to **tell a** .... **lie** than tell the truth and hurt someone.
10 Last month, our bank account was **in the** .... but since that expensive holiday, it's been **in the** ....

SPEAKING

Versions of the truth

The Nigel Benn case has caused bad publicity for the police. Chief Inspector Hunter is investigating what really happened.
The Chief Inspector has called a meeting of the people involved in the case. When your teacher has given you roles, think about what you will say, and then act out the meeting:

- Chief Inspector Hunter
- Nigel Benn
- Ambrose Mendy
- The policeman in the patrol car
- Witness 1: a lorry driver
- Witness 2: a motorist

Try to use as many of the colour idioms as possible from the Vocabulary exercise above.

VOCABULARY

Adjectives of personality

1 Join these split sentences so they make sense.

1	She is incredibly mean;	**a**	she can read and she's only three years old.
2	It isn't fair	**b**	you've already eaten enough.
3	She wasn't sympathetic;	**c**	to write poetry.
4	You have to be sensitive	**d**	this is going to hurt a little.
5	It is extremely cruel	**e**	he sends everyone to sleep.
6	Anna is really bright;	**f**	so she avoids going to parties.
7	Don't be so greedy;	**g**	she just laughed when I told her my problem.
8	Suspicious people	**h**	she has no respect for other people.
9	Try to be brave, Simon;	**i**	to kick the cat.
10	He is so dull	**j**	to jump the queue like that.
11	She's a shy person	**k**	she never buys anyone a coffee.
12	Cathy is so arrogant;	**l**	never believe what you say.

2 Look at the adjectives in the sentences above.

- Which adjectives are the opposite of:
  a generous?
  b trusting?

- Which adjective means:
  c courageous, unafraid of pain or danger?
  d intelligent and lively?
  e nervous in the company of others?
  f extremely unkind?
  g boring?
  h proud and self-important?

- Which adjective is often confused with:
  i sensible?
  j nice?

SPEAKING

Who are you?

1 We can analyse someone's personality by finding out which colours they like.

Study the five coloured circles carefully. Think about how each of the colours makes you feel.
   Now put them in order of preference. For example, if you like the colour yellow the best, then put a 1 by it. If red is your least favourite, then put a 5 by it, and so on. Try to think of the colours simply as colours, not whether they would suit you to wear or whether they are fashionable.

2 Now look at p. 79 and see what your order tells you about your personality!

LANGUAGE STUDY

Different types of description

1 Match the answers (**a–d**) with the questions (**1–4**).

1 What's she like?   a Much better.
2 How is she?   b Reading and playing tennis.
3 What does she like?   c Tall and slim.
4 What does she look like? d Kind.

2 Which question asks about:
a appearance? b preferences? c character? d health?

Which questions can sometimes mean the same?

3 Carmen works in a travel agent's in London. Her aunt is coming to visit her from Spain. Unfortunately Carmen can't go to the airport to meet her aunt, so she rings her fiancé, Roger, who agrees to go instead.
You are going to hear Carmen's side of the telephone conversation. What five things do you think Roger wants to know? Make notes.

NOTES
1 ....
....
2 ....
....
3 ....
....
4 ....
....
5 ....
....

4 This time, listen to both sides of the conversation. Were you right?

SPEAKING

In pairs, take it in turns to imagine that you are in a situation like Carmen's. Your partner has agreed to meet one of your friends or relatives that he/she has never seen before, and to look after your friend/relative for the day.
Remember to ask about appearance, character, likes and dislikes.

	1st	2nd	3rd	4th	5th
BLACK ●	cruel	bad-tempered	mean	easy-going	cheerful
YELLOW ○	sociable	romantic	sympathetic	dull	hard-working
GREEN ●	bright	arrogant	suspicious	practical	greedy
RED ●	aggressive	brave	efficient	fair	shy
BLUE ●	calm	sensitive	generous	lazy	dishonest

DO YOU AGREE WITH THE INTERPRETATION? FIND OUT WHAT YOUR CLASSMATES THINK ALSO.

79

WRITING

The nanny hunt

1 Look at this advertisement which appeared in the *Nanny* magazine.

- Who are the couple looking for?
- What qualities would the ideal person have?

> **Psychologist wife and writer husband** (working at home) desperately seek live-in nanny to take care of three young children aged 6, 5 and nine months. Apply by sending letter and photo. Also put these colours in order of preference – blue, red, green, yellow and black. Send letter and photo to: **Professor and Mr Wallace, 265 Queen Elizabeth Way, London SW15**

2 Before you read the letters, look at the photographs of the three girls and describe them. What do you think they are like as people? Which one looks the most suitable from her photograph?

3 Look at letter **A** carefully. There are over fifteen common mistakes in it. Do your best to correct the letter.

4 Compare letters **B** and **C**.
- Which of the two letters is more appropriate?
- What advice would you give to Sally Fairclough if she showed you her letter before she posted it?
- Make a list of any formal/informal language you can find in the two letters.

5 Look at the colour choices made by each applicant, and at their letters, and decide who Professor Wallace might give the job to.

6 Imagine that you want to apply for a job as a nanny, au pair or butler. Write a letter of application which is friendly but not too informal, telling your potential employers something about yourself. Remember to add your colour preferences!

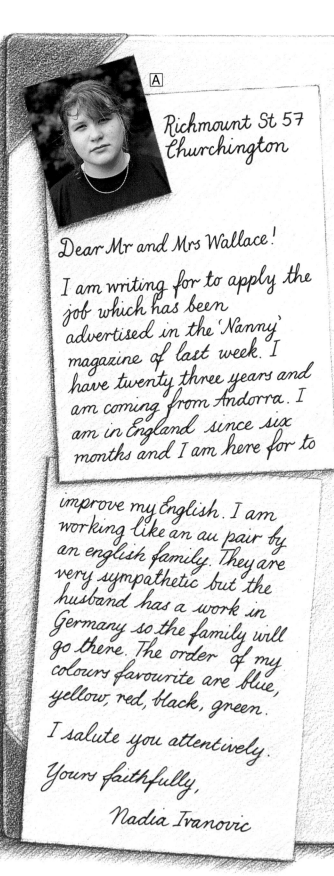

A

Richmount St 57
Churchington

Dear Mr and Mrs Wallace!

I am writing for to apply the job which has been advertised in the 'Nanny' magazine of last week. I have twenty three years and am coming from Andorra. I am in England since six months and I am here for to improve my English. I am working like an au pair by an english family. They are very sympathetic but the husband has a work in Germany so the family will go there. The order of my colours favourite are blue, yellow, red, black, green.

I salute you attentively.
Yours faithfully,

Nadia Ivanovic

B

Dear Mr and Mrs Wallace,

Hello there. I saw your ad. in a magazine and really thought I'd like to apply. I am 19 years old and left school last year. I am working in a clothes shop at the moment, just to fill in. I haven't had any training as a nanny but I love kids and come from a big family. What's more, I could really do with a job! I can start straight away if you like. Here is a photo of me. It would be great if we could have a chat next Friday because I am going to a party in London on Friday evening. I hope to hear from you soon.

Bye for now!

All the best.

Sally Fairclough

PS My favourite colours are yellow, green, red, blue and black.

C

Dear Professor and Mr Wallace,

I am writing in reply to your advertisement in last week's Nanny magazine.

I am a twenty-six-year-old fully-qualified children's nanny and nurse with five years' experience. I have worked for a number of British families and those of the foreign diplomatic community. I can supply you with references if you should require them. I am currently employed as a nanny to two American children but my contract is coming to an end and I am available for interview at your convenience. I could commence a new position almost immediately. I have enclosed a recent photograph.

As requested, my order of preference for the colours you mentioned is black, yellow, red, green and blue.

I look forward to your reply.

Yours sincerely,

Lucy Clinton-Rogers

Lucy Clinton-Rogers

SPEAKING

- How far does the picture match your idea of the typical Englishman?
- How does he feel, and why?

READING

The typical Englishman

Read the paragraph and see if it agrees with your stereotype of the typical Englishman.

The typical Englishman works in a London bank but lives in the countryside, in a house with a lovely garden. Every day he reads the *Times* newspaper and does the crossword on the way to work. He never speaks to anybody on the train, but will talk to you about the weather or cricket if you meet him in the pub at lunchtime. He always wears a dark suit to work and always carries an umbrella.

He gave up smoking his pipe and wearing a bowler hat some years ago. At the weekend, he wears an old tweed jacket and a pair of gardening trousers.

He likes plain, simple food and drinks tea at every opportunity. In his free time, he works in his garden, plays golf or takes his dog for a walk. He is suspicious of all foreigners. He is kind and polite to his wife but does not show her a lot of affection.

His wife is a snob who dresses rather badly. They both admire members of the Royal Family and copy their accents. He is proud of his son, who is at Cambridge University, (but would rather die than tell him). He is rather worried about his daughter, who is currently living with a punk, but hopes that she will eventually marry a doctor or an accountant.

WRITING

National stereotypes

Write a similar paragraph with a stereotypical view of someone from your own country. Then swap them and compare them!

LISTENING

Agreeing and disagreeing

Shirley and Simon are talking about the 'typical Englishman' who has been described in the first paragraph.

1 Listen and answer these questions.

1 Who believes the 'typical Englishman' of the article no longer exists?
2 Why was Simon surprised in the post office?
3 What do they think about the typical English family?
4 Why do they think the British have a poor reputation abroad?

2 Listen again and put the following expressions in the order in which you hear them. Which ones show: full agreement, partial agreement, disagreement?

a Absolutely...
b Alright, but...
c That's right
d That's just not true...
e You're right

SPEAKING

We're all different!

1 Draw a map of your country and its main cities. If people from a particular area or city have a reputation for being shy, write 'shy' beside it. Try to use some of the adjectives you looked at in Set B of this Unit.

2 When you have finished, talk about your map with a partner. Your partner must agree or disagree with you!

READING | **1** Look at the photo and headline for the newspaper article. What do you think the article will be about?
Read the article quickly and check your predictions.

THE GENDER TRAP

ARE YOU FOREIGN, AGED BETWEEN 17 AND 27 AND UNMARRIED? If so, have you thought of getting a job as an au pair? It's a great way of spending a year in England. You stay with an English family and, in return for housework and babysitting, you get food and accommodation and a little pocket money. You can also pick up a lot of English. However, there's a catch! It doesn't really matter where you're from, but you have to be female, as several male au pairs have found out, the hard way.

25-year-old Arnie, from Iceland, was taken on to look after four-year-old Sam. Arnie is ideal: he's great with Sam - he bathes him and picks him up from nursery and has even helped with painting and decorating. Nevertheless, the authorities want to kick him out because he's a man. English law says that only girls are allowed to be au pairs.

This isn't the first case of sex discrimination. Two years ago, Hoken Larsson from Sweden was turned away at immigration, despite being the ideal man for the job. Of course, if he had had an EC passport, probably nothing would have happened. In theory, he still wouldn't have been able to work, but nobody would have checked. The divorcee who had wanted to employ him said that her eight-year-old son needed a male presence about the house. Understandably, Hoken was furious: 'What do they want me to do,' he asked angrily, 'put on a skirt and wear a wig? It's ridiculous!' He wished he had known about these regulations before coming all the way to England.

Maria Mirkova, who heads an au-pair agency, would disagree with Hoken. 'How could a boy be an au pair? A girl can take far better care of a two-year-old baby than a boy - he has different instincts about feeding; she's better equipped to do the housework.'

2 Now read the article closely and decide whether these statements are **true** or **false**.

1 English girls can work as au pairs in England.
2 Arnie is still in England.
3 Hoken never started his job.
4 Hoken knew about the regulations for au pairs before coming to England.
5 Maria Mirkova believes that boys can be good au pairs.

3 How far do you agree with Maria Mirkova?

LANGUAGE STUDY

The third conditional and **wish**

1 Look at this sentence from the text.

*If he **had had** an EC passport, probably nothing **would have** happened.*
If + had + PAST PARTICIPLE

This construction is usually called the THIRD CONDITIONAL.
Now study this way of expressing regret about the past.

*He **wished** he **had known** about these regulations…*
Wished + had + PAST PARTICIPLE

What similarities do you notice between this construction and the third conditional?

2 **Practice**
Make two sentences around each of these mini-situations, one using the third conditional and one using **wished**.

1 Alan was lazy at school. He didn't pass his exams.
2 Caroline drank too much champagne last night. Now she has a terrible headache.
3 The policemen who stopped Nigel Benn got into trouble with their inspector.

SPEAKING

A woman's place

1 Look at this list of jobs. In pairs, decide which ones are usually done by men and which are usually done by women. Which ones could be done by both?

soldier	secretary	teacher	doctor	taxi-driver
mechanic	carpenter	air steward		lorry driver
nurse	coal miner	bullfighter		shop assistant
au pair	boxer	accountant	cook	hairdresser

2 In your country, which of these jobs would only be done by men?

3 People used to say: 'A woman's place is in the home.' How popular do you think this view was or is in your country?

When in Rome

SPEAKING

Could you eat it?

Going to different countries often means getting used to food which is very different from your own.

Look at these dishes. Which countries do they come from?

| sheep's eyes   snails   snake   veal cooked in milk   dog   birds' nests |
| toad-in-the-hole   tripe and onions   brains   raw fish   horse   turtle |

Which ones could you never eat, even if you were starving?

Are there any dishes in your country which you know most foreigners wouldn't try?

LISTENING

Toad-in-the-hole!

Poppy is meeting Martin Smith, her father's friend, and Martin's wife, Moira at a traditional English restaurant in Covent Garden.

1 Look at the menu. (Your teacher will explain any items you don't understand.) Then listen and make a note of what each person decides to order.

2 Listen again and write down the exact words Moira uses when she
- decides what to eat
- tells Poppy what she has decided to order.

The Hot Pot Traditional English Restaurant

Starters · all at £4.50
Smoked salmon
Avocado pear & prawns
Watercress soup
Cheese & onion tart

Main Courses · all at £7.00

Meat
Grilled lamb chops in a mint sauce
Roast Beef & Yorkshire pudding
Duck in orange sauce
Toad-in-the-hole

Fish
Grilled sole
Salmon fillet baked in pastry

All main courses served with vegetables

Desserts · all at £3.50
Apple pie & cream
Bread-and-butter pudding
Luxury ice-creams

Cheese selection · £3.50

All prices include VAT 12½% service charge

LANGUAGE STUDY

Going to or will?

1 **Going to** has two main uses:

● to talk about future plans and events which have already been decided:
I'm going to be a policeman when I grow up. (I decided this years ago.)

● as a way of predicting something you can actually see is going to happen:
'Look at that fat lady, Mummy.'
'She's not fat, darling; she's going to have a baby.'

2 Match the examples using **will** with the definitions of their use.

1 Will you open the door for me?   **a** An expression of determination.
2 If you do that again, I'll be very angry.   **b** A spontaneous decision/offer.
3 I will go to the disco if I want to, Dad.   **c** A prediction.
4 Don't worry, I'll give you a lift.   **d** A condition, threat or promise.
5 You will marry a tall stranger.   **e** After verbs like, think, hope, doubt…
6 I hope she'll believe me.   **f** An order/request.

3 Now look at the tapescript for the conversation in the listening exercise. Can you explain the use of **will** and **going to**?

4 Look at the following situations and decide what you would say in each. There may be more than one possible answer.

1 It is 3 a.m. Some people are making a lot of noise in front of your house. What do you say to them as a warning before you call the police?
2 The sky is full of dark clouds. Your friend suggests a game of tennis. What do you reply?
3 You see an old person trying to lift a heavy suitcase onto a train. What do you say when you want to help?
4 You are determined to lose three kilos before your next summer holiday. What do you say to yourself?
5 You don't know what to buy your father for his birthday.
Suddenly you have a brilliant idea! What do you say to yourself? And then…
6 what do you tell your mother?

SPEAKING

Role play

Imagine you are on holiday in England and you go to the Hot Pot Restaurant. In groups of four, act out a situation where three of you are customers and the fourth is the waiter.

WRITING

Making a menu

Make up a typical menu from your country. Decide how you will explain the dishes to your customers. Perhaps you could write the explanations on the menu itself.

VOCABULARY

Cooking

1 Match the words in the box with the pictures in the word map opposite.

to mix   to boil   a frying pan   to roast   to bake   to slice   to fry   to stir   a pot
a bowl   to spread   a dish   to chop   a saucepan   to sprinkle   to beat   to grill

2 Can you add any more words?

3 What is the difference between these three things: *receipt, prescription, recipe*?

LISTENING

You are going to hear how to make a famous traditional English dish: 'Bread-and-Butter Pudding'.

1 Listen carefully and make notes under these headings:

Ingredients	Utensils	Method
....	....	....
....	....	....
....	....	....
....	....	....
....	....	....
....	....	....
....	....	....
....	....	....
....	....	....
....	....	....

2 Look at the tapescript on p. 155 and check if you missed anything.

WRITING

Using the tapescript as a guide, write a simple recipe for a dish from your country.

COOKERY

ACTIONS

CUTTING

A

B

PREPARING

C

D

E

F

COOKING

G

H

I

J

K

L

EQUIPMENT

M

N

O

P

Q

89

LISTENING

Watch your body language

Dr Ian Williams is being interviewed about the different meanings gestures can have.

1 What caused the misunderstanding in India?
2 What universal European gesture does he mention?
3 What do the gestures mean in the countries which are mentioned?

a North Europe
Greece and Italy

b Italy
France
Greece
Spain

LANGUAGE STUDY

Remember, forget and remind

1 Remember and forget

What is the difference between the uses of **remember** in these two sentences taken from the conversation?

a *I remember going to India.*
b *...remember to keep your hands in your pockets.*

Notice that (**not**) **forget to** can be used in the same way as **remember to**:

...don't forget to keep your hands in your pockets.

2 Remind

If you **remind someone to do something**, you are helping them to remember.

3 Complete the sentences using an appropriate form of **remember**, **remind** or **forget**.

1 Can you .... me to post this letter?
2 I can't find my car keys, but I .... seeing them here earlier.
3 Oh, dear! It's his birthday and I've .... to buy him a present!
4 Do you think you could .... me how to use the photocopier?
5 Don't .... to ask for a receipt.
6 .... to be back by 11.00, otherwise there will be trouble!
7 I .... overtaking the lorry, but everything afterwards is a blank.
8 Always .... to get good travel insurance when you go abroad.

READING

Keep your hands in your pockets!

This is an extract from a humorous advertisement for Heathrow, London's most important airport, where people of all nationalities and cultures meet. In it, Desmond Morris talks about the problems associated with different nationalities' body language. Here, he looks at a few misunderstandings which could occur.

1 Find out what the 'ring gesture' means to:
   an American, a Japanese, a Tunisian, a Frenchman, a Colombian.
2 Why does the Colombian choke on his wine?
3 Why is the Syrian insulted?
4 How does the poor waiter get stabbed?

Is there at least one truly international gesture? Don't bet on it!

A Japanese asks an American passenger whether Heathrow has a luggage trolley service. It has. And as it happens, this service is not only first class, but FREE! So the Yank replies with the famous 'A-OK' ring gesture. But to the Japanese this signifies 'money' and he concludes there is a charge for the service. Meanwhile, a Tunisian on-looker thinks the American is telling the Japanese that he is a worthless rogue and he is going to kill him.

The ring gesture can have further meanings …

A Frenchman has just read a British Airport Authorities advertisement. Glancing round the restaurant in Terminal 4, he remarks wonderingly to his wife, 'You know how much zis airport cost the British taxpayer? Not a sou.' And he makes the finger-and-thumb ring, which to him means 'zero'.

Unfortunately, at the same time, he is glancing at a Colombian who is enjoying a fine Burgundy with his steak Bearnaise. The Colombian, enraged by the deadly obscenity which he assumes is directed at him, chokes on his wine and catches his nose with finger and thumb. This appalls a Syrian opposite, who thinks the Colombian is telling him to 'go to hell'. The Syrian is restrained with difficulty by his Greek colleague from getting up and punching the Colombian on the nose. Meanwhile the *maitre d'* hurries over and attempts to calm the situation with two out-thrust palms. This of course is taken by the Greek to be a double 'moutza' and, in his rage, he promptly skewers the unfortunate man with his fish-knife.

SPEAKING

Just good manners

Below is some advice for travellers to Japan and to Arab countries.

1 Work in pairs. One of you should read about Japan while the other reads about Arab countries.

2 When you have finished, look at the pictures and explain to each other the social rules which have been broken in each one.

3 Now read the article you haven't yet looked at. Is there anything your partner forgot to tell you?

4 Go through the texts and underline all the useful words and expressions which are used to express what you **must** and **mustn't** do.
Make a list of them.

LANGUAGE STUDY

In case

1 In the text about Japan, it says:

*You shouldn't sit on tables **in case** you offend someone.*

= You should avoid sitting on a table because you might offend someone if you do.

Never kiss people as a greeting; shake hands or bow instead. Always take off your shoes when you go into someone's flat. Never blow your nose in public – the Japanese find this quite shocking.

You shouldn't sit on tables in case you offend someone. When you take a bath, make sure that you wash with soap *before* you get into the bath. Whatever you do never use soap *in* the bath itself; the bath is just for relaxation.

Don't expect to be invited to Japanese homes. Most entertaining is done in restaurants and clubs. Be prepared to drink a lot! Don't be shocked if Japanese people drink soup noisily; this is perfectly acceptable in Japan and is not considered bad manners.

Traditionally, the Japanese are great gift-givers and it is common, and a sign of respect, to exchange presents, so make sure you have a selection of typical gifts from your country in case you need them.

22

We use **in case** + PRESENT SIMPLE to talk about things we do now in order to prevent problems later.

*I'll take a map **in case** I get lost.* (Because if I *do* get lost, I won't be able to find my way without a map.)

2 Now re-write these sentences using **in case** <u>where possible</u>.

1 I'll take my coat because the weather may change.
2 I think I'll buy a thick paperback. I may have to wait a long time at the airport.
3 Cash often gets stolen, so I'll take some traveller's cheques.
4 I'd better take some tablets because I often get seasick.
5 I'll travel to Majorca if I can get a flight.

WRITING

An advice sheet for foreigners

1 Imagine that you are preparing an advice sheet for visitors to your country.

Make a list of things that visitors to your country
- **should/must** do.
- **shouldn't/mustn't** do.

2 Now decide which ones are the most/least important.

3 Using the texts you have read as a model, write an advice sheet for visitors to your country.

Customs do vary, but on the whole these rules are true for all Arab countries. Travellers should always dress modestly. Don't wear shorts. Men should always wear shirts. Women should cover their arms and never walk around in sun dresses. It is wise to carry a scarf with you in case you need to cover your hair.

Arabs are hospitable and may invite you home. Take off your shoes when you enter the home. Even if alcohol is offered stick to tea or soft drinks. In some countries men and women eat in separate rooms.

Men shouldn't expect to meet the female members of the host's family and don't take them flowers. People usually sit on cushions or mattresses on the ground. It is bad manners to stretch out your legs and show the soles of your feet.

Traditionally, meals are eaten from a communal dish using the fingers. **Never** pick up food with your left hand as this is considered disgusting.

23

Rise and Fall

SPEAKING

New Found Land

1 A large island has been discovered. An international community of 10,000 men and women are going to start a new country there. Imagine that you have to decide the laws of the new country. Discuss the following questions.

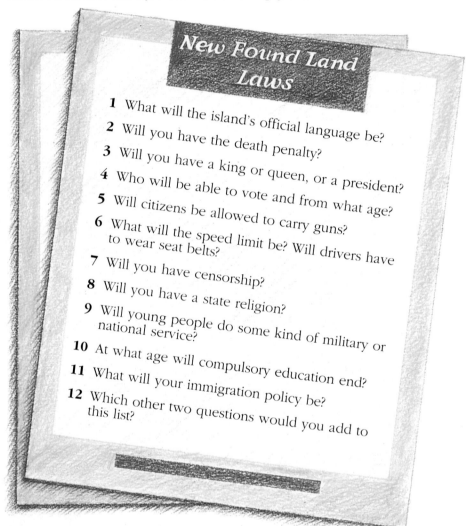

New Found Land Laws

1 What will the island's official language be?

2 Will you have the death penalty?

3 Will you have a king or queen, or a president?

4 Who will be able to vote and from what age?

5 Will citizens be allowed to carry guns?

6 What will the speed limit be? Will drivers have to wear seat belts?

7 Will you have censorship?

8 Will you have a state religion?

9 Will young people do some kind of military or national service?

10 At what age will compulsory education end?

11 What will your immigration policy be?

12 Which other two questions would you add to this list?

2 Speakers' Corner

Speakers' Corner is a part of Hyde Park, in London, where people are free to say whatever they like.

Two or three people in your class should choose the question from the list above that they feel most strongly about. They should stand in separate parts of the class and start talking about their point of view. The rest of the class can move from person to person. Feel free to disagree and interrupt!

VOCABULARY

Geography

Study the words in the box and look up any meanings you are unsure of. Make as many connections as you can between the various words.

Example: *A stream is a small river.*
You would probably find a swamp in the jungle.

sea	jungle	harbour	desert	waterfall	forest	hill	coral	coast
pool	spring	mountain	oasis	river	plain	swamp	beach	wave
bay	stream	port	valley	lake	tide	wood	island	plateau

READING

Describing a country's geography

1 Which two countries are described below? Can you guess?

A A country in E Asia covering vast areas of land, ranging from the low-lying and densely populated plains of the NE to the high peaks of the Tibetan Plateau in the W, rising well over 5000 m (16,500 ft). In the far NW, much of the land is desert or semi-desert. The country falls into three regions around its three main rivers: the Yellow River in the N, the Yangtze in the centre and the Xi Jiang in the S.

B A country in NW South America, lying on the Equator, from which it takes its name. It includes the Galapagos Islands 1000 km (600 miles) out in the Pacific. It consists chiefly of a coastal plain in the W, separated from the tropical jungles and rivers of the Amazon Basin (Oriente) by ranges and plateaux of the Andes (containing several active volcanoes, including Cotopaxi). There are frequent disastrous earthquakes.

2 Make notes on the countries under these headings:

NAME	LOCATION	GEOGRAPHICAL FEATURES
....	....	....
....	....	....
....	....	....

SPEAKING

The newest continent

Work in pairs to complete the maps of the main sights of Australia.

STUDENT A look at the map on p. 138.   **STUDENT B** look at the map on p. 142.

WRITING

My own country

Use the headings from exercise 2 above and make notes about your country. Then write a short description of it.

READING
Discover Australia

Read the advertisement in the brochure and decide if the following statements are **true** or **false**.

1 Someone will meet you when you arrive in Sydney.
2 You will spend a whole day touring Sydney.
3 The Featherdale Wildlife Park is in Alice Springs.
4 You will fly from Alice Springs to Palm Valley.
5 You will be able to ride a camel at the Virginia Camel Farm.
6 The Olgas are valleys.
7 You will see the sunset over the Olgas.
8 You can see crocodiles in the Kakadu National Park.
9 The Wangi Falls are above the rainforest.
10 You'll see tropical fish from the catamaran.

LANGUAGE STUDY
Uses of **a/an, the** and **some**

Study these rules and then decide if the sentences which follow are right or wrong.

a/an
We use **a/an** (the indefinite article)
- before singular countable nouns when we are talking about *one* of something in a general, non-specific way.
  *We saw **a** kangaroo from our landrover.*
- when referring to somebody's job or profession
  *She's **a** travel agent.*

We do not use **a**
- before plural nouns (e.g. *kangaroos*)
- before uncountable nouns like *oil, sugar* and *water*.
- before abstract nouns or nouns expressing concepts like *love, art, weather*.

Discover Australia in 14 days

DAY 1 Arrive in **Sydney**. Make your own way to the **Central Plaza Hotel**.

DAY 2 A full day touring **Sydney**, including a cruise around the magnificent harbour. Your tour includes the Opera House, colourful King's Cross, famous Bondi Beach, Double Bay and cross the Harbour Bridge.

DAY 3 Tour through the picturesque **Blue Mountains**. Visit the Featherdale Wildlife Park where kangaroos and koalas (you can cuddle one!) can be seen.

DAY 4 Fly to **Alice Springs**. Tour of Alice this afternoon.

DAY 5 Travel by special 4WD vehicle through the colourful mountain ranges into **Palm Valley** where unique plants of a species thousands of years old still survive. Superb oasis scenery.

DAY 6 On the way to **Ayer's Rock**, call at the Virginia Camel Farm. There's time for a camel ride. This afternoon see the nearby Olgas (twenty-eight domes of rock that dominate the western skyline) returning in time to see the sunset over Ayer's Rock.

DAY 7 View sunrise on **Ayer's Rock**. 7.15 start for those wishing to climb. In the caves beneath the rock, find out about

the aboriginals 'dream time' mythology, or simply tour around the base of this monolith. Return to **Alice Springs**.

DAY 8 Fly to **Darwin** where you will transfer to your hotel.

DAY 9 Travel to **Kakadu National Park**. Watch out for wildlife as we make our way to Cooinda and Yellow Waters Billabong. Enjoy an exciting boat cruise to observe the crocodiles and birdlife.

the

We use **the** (the definite article)

- before uncountable nouns and singular and plural countable nouns when we move from the general to the specific
  *We saw a kangaroo from our landrover. **The** kangaroo was running fast. In fact, all **the** animals were running fast.*
  *I'm thirsty – where's **the** water?*

- before some place names (but not usually towns, cities or countries) and geographical/ environmental features
  *We saw **the** Olgas/**the** coast.*

- when we are talking about a species or a class
  ***The** kangaroo is an interesting creature.*

- before superlatives
  ***The** best, **the** most interesting...*

DAY 10 Visit **Ubirr Rock** and see many aboriginal rock drawings and paintings.

DAY 11 A sandstone plateau forms the Tabletop Range. Close to its edge, springs and streams form rock pools which tumble as the **Wangi Falls** into the rainforest below

DAY 12 Fly to **Cairns** today. Transfer to your hotel.

DAY 13 Cruise to the **Great Barrier Reef**, including the outer reef. Travel by air-conditioned catamaran. There's time for swimming, snorkelling and coral viewing. See shoals of tropical fish from a sub-sea vessel. Lunch, glass-bottom boat ride included.

DAY 14 Depart from **Cairns**. End of tour.

We do not use **the**

- before plural countable nouns if we are talking about something in general
  I like koala bears.

some

We use **some**

- before uncountable nouns and plural countable nouns if we are describing something that we can see or that exists.
  *There are **some** koala bears over there.*

Are these sentences right or wrong?
1 Tourists love kangaroos.
2 He's learning to be sheep farmer.
3 The most visitors to Australia love the climate.
4 Kakadu is the most amazing place I've visited.
5 Is it true that Australian men hate art?
6 The leaves are its favourite food.
7 She's studying the koala bear.
8 There's a letter from Sydney for you.
9 There's always a beautiful weather on Hawaii.
10 Sea there is lovely and warm.

LISTENING

The world's favourite Australians

1 Listen to the talk about Australian wildlife.

1 Tick what is special about the duck-billed platypus.
  a It has toes.
  b It has fur.
  c It has feathers.
  d It gives birth to its young.
  e It is cold-blooded, like a snake.

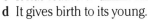

2 Here is one unusual thing about the koala bear.
  - It is active at night.   Find two others.

3 Name the koala bear's enemies:
  a two hundred years ago.
  b about seventy years ago.
  c nowadays.

4 How friendly are koalas?

5 What does 'koala' mean?

2 Look at the tapescript on pp. 155–6 and notice when the definite and indefinite articles are used. Some are in bold type. Can you explain their use?

READING | Xingu, the forbidden area

The singer Sting visited the Brazilian rainforest with the writer J.P. Dutilleux. Here is an extract from the book they wrote.

1 Look at the picture of Sting with the Indian chief Raoni and describe them. What do you think the rainforest is like? How dangerous do you think it would be in the rainforest?

2 Now read the text and answer these two questions.

1 Why, and for whom, is Xingu a forbidden area?
2 How does the rainforest look from the air?

Now that we are out of the clouds, we can see the land below us stretching to the horizon. It's a desert of red dust. J.P. looks sad.

'All of this was rainforest ten years ago,' says J.P. 'A few isolated tree stumps are left to remind us of what used to be there. This is the kind of devastation only men can cause. I feel angry for my children and their children, being robbed of the earth's beauty for the sake of dirty money.'

'We lose 100 species of plant and animal every day,' says our guide. 'Who knows, a cure for AIDS or cancer could have existed down there just waiting to be discovered, it's a living laboratory. But what do we do? We burn it all down. It's criminal.'

'So why doesn't someone do something about it?'

'Look, Sting, this is the last frontier. You are visiting a place that very few white people have ever seen. No president of Brazil has ever visited this area. We can't depend on anyone else. Each person that comes here has to take responsibility. Look there's the Indian border.'

The sight below us is remarkable. The wasteland suddenly ends in a wall of gigantic forest. Two planets have been put side by side. A dead and devastated world, cheek-to-cheek with a world of green beauty and life, the Xingu.

'Where the Indians are, the forest is protected, and where they aren't, it is not. That's why the Indians are systematically being wiped out.'

There used to be six million Indians in the Amazon Basin. Now there are only two hundred thousand. They've been killed, sometimes by guns, sometimes by blankets carrying disease dropped on villages, destroyed by alcohol and the demoralization of their culture.

'How big is the protected area of the Xingu?'

'It's about the size of Belgium. It's a showpiece. The tribe we're visiting are a peaceful tribe, but they are protected by the hostile tribes of the Lower Xingu of which Raoni is the chief.'

'How hostile?' J.P. doesn't answer.

A straight highway from north to south has been cut through the thick forest … the Trans-Amazonian highway. Traffic is not allowed to stop. Anyone who entered the forest would be killed by Indian patrols.

We all suddenly realize we're not entering Disneyland. J.P. just smiles.

3 Make answers to the questions and questions for the answers.

1 Why is J.P. so angry?
2 ....? – One hundred a day.
3 Why does J.P. call the rainforest a 'living laboratory'?
4 How are the Indians being killed?
5 ....? – Some are peaceful, some are hostile.
6 ....? – The chief of the hostile tribes.
7 Why is the Xingu not like Disneyland?

LANGUAGE STUDY

The passive

*'They **are protected** by the hostile tribes of the Lower Xingu.'*

1 Study these two sentences and how they are both formed.

a ACTIVE *A crocodile ate the explorer.*
      SUBJECT+VERB+OBJECT

b PASSIVE *The explorer was eaten by a crocodile.*
      SUBJECT + to be + PAST + AGENT
                   PARTICIPLE

1 What happens to the verb when you change the sentence from active to passive?
2 What happens to the object of sentence **a** in sentence **b**?
3 What happens to the subject of sentence **a** in sentence **b**?

Note: If the subject of the active sentence is not important because the emphasis is on the verb (the action) or the object (who/what the action is happening to), the passive sentence does not contain an agent.

2 Rewrite the following sentences, converting the verbs from **active** to *passive* or *passive* to **active**. Identify the tense in each case.

1 The Indians **protect** the forests.
2 The Indians *are being wiped out* by guns and disease.
3 Children *will be robbed* of the earth's beauty by human greed.
4 Very few white people **have seen** this place.
5 Alcohol **destroyed** thousands of Indians.

WRITING

Writing a summary

Using your own words (maximum number in brackets), continue the following sentences to make a summary of the rainforest text.

The destruction of the rainforest is a tragedy because... *(30 words)*
The Indian population has fallen because... *(30 words)*
The Xingu is protected so that... *(20 words)*
It's dangerous for strangers to go into the Xingu because... *(20 words)*

LISTENING

Don't be so green!

Maria, from Brazil, is a postgraduate student in England. She is discussing practical ways to save the rainforest.

1 Listen for answers to these questions:

1 Why, according to Maria, are poor countries encouraged to destroy the environment?
2 What does she accuse rich countries of doing?
3 How much did Frank pay for his jar of instant coffee?
4 How much stays in the coffee-producing country?
5 What happens to the rest of the money?

2 How far do you agree with what Maria says? How far does Frank accept the responsibility which developed countries have? Who wins their discussion?

VOCABULARY

Verbs with prepositions

1 Match the halves to form complete sentences.

1 You blame someone **for** doing something	**a** when you think something is a bad idea.
2 You thank someone **for** doing something	**b** when he/she has done something wrong.
3 You congratulate someone **on** doing something	**c** when you think it's his/her fault.
4 You accuse someone **of** doing something	**d** when you're grateful.
5 You prevent someone **from** doing something	**e** when he/she has done something well.

2 Now use the correct combination of verb and preposition to expand the following sentences.

1 He/blame/government/cut down/trees.
2 He/thank/Indians/welcome/him/to their village.
3 He/congratulate/local people/protect/their forests.
4 He accuse/politicians/not understand/problem.
5 The politicians/prevent/Indians/live/traditional way.

WRITING

Describing a process

1 Put the verbs in brackets into the passive and then put sentences **a – h** in the right order to describe how instant coffee is made. Use the picture to help you.

Coffee is grown in a warm climate but the beans are exported to make instant coffee.

a This coffee (spray) into hot air.
b When they arrive at their destination, the beans (buy) by a coffee dealer and (sell) to a coffee processor.
c The hot air evaporates the water and coffee powder (leave) and freeze-dried.
d The 'cherries', each containing two coffee beans, (pick) and (dry) in the sun.
e These imported coffee beans (roast) and (grind).
f When dry, the beans (separate) from their shells, (put) into sacks and (export).
g When trees are several years old, they flower and (produce) green berries which ripen into 'cherries'.
h In order to produce instant coffee powder, huge pots of fresh coffee (make).

2 Think of a product from your country. Write a short text describing how it is made.

3 Finish the second sentence so that it means the same as the sentence above it.

1 Factories pollute rivers and lakes.
Rivers and lakes ....
2 Fire destroyed the forest.
The forest ....
3 Many countries were affected by the nuclear explosion.
The nuclear explosion ....
4 Thousands of sea birds are killed by oil from tankers.
Oil from tankers ....
5 Gases have damaged the ozone layer...
The ozone layer ....
6 ...so more people will probably be killed by skin cancer.
...so skin cancer ....
7 Some countries have been affected by changes in the weather.
Changes in the weather ....

101

Dog Eat Dog

VOCABULARY

Newspapers

1 Complete the words in the following sentences.

1 The *E* .... is the person in charge of a newspaper.
2 *J* .... are people who write and report for newspapers.
3 The *h* .... of the main story are always on the front page of the newspaper in big letters.
4 A newspaper contains lots of stories or *ar* ....
5 A 'scoop' is an *ex* .... story which one paper reports before any of the others.
6 In Britain, there are two main types of newspapers: the '*p* .... papers' often make news stories more sensational; the '*qu* .... papers' are more serious.
7 In some countries, *c* .... exists; this means that the government decides what the newspapers contain.

2 Find out from each other which types of newspapers your classmates or their families read.

LISTENING

How to get an interview

1 Listen to the conversation and work out who the people in the photographs are.

2 Listen again and think about these questions.

1 Why did the journalist go to the West Indies?
2 What was the journalist's big problem?
3 How did he get round it?
4 Was it a fair way of getting an interview?

3 Look at the tapescript on p. 156 and find the different ways in which **get** is used.

4 **Stress and intonation** 🔲
Listen to this extract. How and why is the stress of the third sentence different?

ANNABEL: You know Oliver Reed?
JULIAN: The film director?
ANNABEL: That's Oliver Stone. Oliver Reed, the actor.

Now listen to this extract. Mark the stress showing where Annabel contradicts and corrects Julian.

ANNABEL: ...he married a schoolgirl.
JULIAN: Who, Wensley what's-his-name?
ANNABEL: No, Oliver Reed.
JULIAN: What! He must have been twice her age!
ANNABEL: Three times, actually.

In pairs, practise saying the two extracts.

SPEAKING

Getting the facts straight

There is a revolution in the capital of Moronia. Journalist Kit Lucas is there for the *Daily Planet* newspaper and is on the phone to the Editor in London. Work in pairs.

STUDENT A You are Kit Lucas. Turn to p. 139.

STUDENT B You are the Editor of the *Daily Planet*. Turn to p. 143.

VOCABULARY

Understanding the headlines

1 The words used in newspaper headlines are often short and dramatic. Match each headline word with its synonym on the right.

a	**ROW**	1	leave/resign
b	**AXE**	2	get married
c	**RIFT**	3	cut
d	**DRAMA**	4	break/division
e	**WED**	5	question/interrogate
f	**BLAZE**	6	exciting event
g	**QUIZ**	7	anger
h	**FURY**	8	argue/argument
i	**QUIT**	9	fire

2 Headlines use a characteristic 'grammar', too. Look at these two examples.

Princess to wed pop idol

= The princess is going to marry a pop star.
The INFINITIVE is used to talk about the future.

Boss axes 1,000 jobs

= The owner has cut 1,000 jobs at his business.
The PRESENT SIMPLE is used to talk about the past.

3 Study these headlines and put them into ordinary English. Think of stories behind the headlines.

1 **MINISTER TO AXE HOSPITALS**
2 **ROYAL COUPLE SAYS NO TO RIFT RUMOUR**
3 **FIRE CHIEF TO QUIT AFTER BLAZE DRAMA**
4 **POLICE QUIZ TEACHER IN EXAM ROW**
5 **FURY AS GOVERNMENT RIFT WIDENS**
6 **PRINCESS WEDS IN PALACE DRAMA**

4 Invent a headline of your own and tell the story behind it.

READING

The scoop!

Wensley Clarkson waited outside Paul and Linda McCartney's deserted country house for an interview.

1 Read the text and discuss which title would best describe the story:

a How to make the truth interesting.
b Anything for a story.
c Journalists are liars.

Perhaps you can invent a better title of your own.

2 Match what actually happened (1–5) with the journalist's account (a–e). Example: 1–e

1 The journalist said: 'I can see from both of you that these marriage rift stories are untrue.'
2 Paul said: 'Load of nonsense.'
3 The journalist said: 'I suppose you wish these gossips would stop.'
4 The journalist asked: 'Would you call them muckspreaders?'
5 The journalist did not ask Paul about the court case in Germany.

a Paul angrily denied rumours of a rift in their fourteen-year marriage.
b Paul was tight-lipped about the court case.
c Paul said: 'We are targets again for these malicious muckspreaders.'
d Paul said: 'I just wish these gossips would go away and stop talking rubbish.'
e Paul insisted: 'I want the world to know that Linda and I are as happy as ever.'

The electric window slid down and with that inimitable smile known to millions, he asked me: 'Yes, what can I do for you?' It was a very relaxed approach when you consider it was almost midnight in a lonely country lane – and for all he knew, I could have been a nutter with a gun. I was so shocked he was talking to me that I hesitated for a moment, then told him who I was. He seemed relieved and I grabbed at that opportunity.

'I can see from both of you that these marriage rift stories aren't true.'

'Yep. Load of nonsense,' came the reply from my genial Liverpudlian host.

'I suppose you wish these gossips would stop,' I carried on.

'Yep. Sure do,' came the next reply.

'Would you call them muckspreaders?' I added.

'Yep.'

'These rumours first surfaced a year ago. They're obviously no more truthful now than then.' I was pushing my luck at this stage.

'Yep. Now why don't you go off home?'

It was my turn to say 'Yep' because that signalled the end of the interview.

Two days later, readers of the *Sunday Mirror* were treated to a marvellous page-three 'Exclusive' headlined 'PAUL'S FURY AT LOVE RIFT LIES' The opening paragraphs read:

Superstar Paul McCartney has hit back at the rumours that his marriage is on the rocks.

'I want the world to know that Linda and I are as happy as ever,' he insisted. 'I just wish these gossips would go away and stop talking rubbish.'

Paul, 40, was speaking on the eve of a West German court case in which a 20-year-old girl, who says she is his illegitimate daughter, is claiming millions of pounds' maintenance from him. He was tight-lipped about the court case – but with Linda by his side he angrily denied show business rumours of a rift in their fourteen-year marriage.

'We're targets once again for these malicious muckspreaders,' he said.

'Last time these rumours started was about a year ago and they are no more truthful how than they were then.'

Paul spoke exclusively to the *Sunday Mirror* at his cottage in the East Sussex countryside, near Rye.

LANGUAGE STUDY
Reporting verbs

1 *'I want the world to know that Linda and I are as happy as ever,'* he **insisted**.

The following example shows how the reporting verb **insist** can be used to put the sentence into reported speech.

*Paul **insisted (that)** he and Linda were as happy as ever.*

2 Reporting verbs use these following patterns.

1 *He **insisted** (that) **they were** happy.*
   VERB1 + that + someone + VERB 2

2 *She **persuaded him to tell** the truth.*
   VERB 1 + someone + INFINITIVE (with to)

Other verbs: **advise, ask, encourage, persuade, remind, tell, warn**

3 *He **denied** stealing the handbag.*
   VERB 1 + VERB 2 + ing + (something)

Other verbs: **admit, suggest**

4 *His teacher **suggested** (that) **he should become** a journalist.*   suggest (that) + someone + should + INFINITIVE (without to) + something

3 Put these sentences into reported speech using the reporting verb at the beginning of the second sentence.

1 'If I were you I wouldn't print that story,' he said.
   He advised me ....
2 'I didn't take those photographs!' she said.
   She denied ....
3 'Please don't print my name,' she said.
   She asked me ....
4 'Don't give him an interview!' he warned me.
   He warned me ....
5 'I invented the story,' Julian said.
   Julian admitted ....
6 'Why don't you phone the editor?' he said.
   He suggested ....
7 'Get a photograph of the accident,' she said to her secretary.
   The editor told ....
8 'Tell me what happened,' he said. I did.
   He persuaded ....

READING | Tricked!

You are going to read two newspaper articles about two English girls who were arrested for smuggling rare birds' eggs.

1 Work in pairs. One of you reads article **A** while the other reads article **B** on the opposite page.

Answer as many questions as you can, then exchange information with your partner. (*Don't worry* if you can't understand all the vocabulary.)

1 Where is Kathy from?
2 What is special about the eggs?
3 How much did they weigh?
4 How does Kathy feel now?

5 Where were the eggs hidden?
6 What was the girls' destination?
7 Who else was involved?
8 What penalties does each girl face?

Too naive for this world?

Hot tears ran down the cheeks of Oxford girl KATHY GRAHAM as she tried to reach out to touch me through the bars of her cell. 'Why was I such a fool?' she cried, her whole body shaken by heartrending sobs. 'I'll go crazy if I have to stay in this place,' she screamed. What started out as a luxury holiday for Kathy (18) and a friend has turned into a nightmare!

Kathy is told she faces a long prison sentence if she is found guilty of trying to smuggle six priceless parrot eggs out of a small Caribbean state whose government is determined to prevent the bird from dying out. (Only 50 female birds are known to exist.) A top professor has been arrested in connection with the eggs' disappearance. Kathy's friend Jennifer, who isn't yet 18, will probably escape with deportation.

'I know people won't believe us, but we were taken in, tricked, by people we thought were our friends. We didn't have a clue what we were carrying,' said Kathy, one minute laughing hysterically, the next in floods of tears.

Perhaps next month's trial will help us to get to the bottom of this story.

Two women arrested for smuggling 'chocolates'

TWO YOUNG WOMEN are awaiting trial in the Caribbean after being arrested for trying to smuggle out rare eggs of a near-extinct parrot.

One of the women, 18-year-old Kathy Graham, spoke from the cell where she is being held in custody, saying that she saw herself not as a criminal but as a victim. She had been tricked, she said, by 'professional' smugglers.

Kathy and a friend, Jennifer Roberts, were about to fly to London when they were stopped by suspicious customs officers who discovered six eggs weighing just 12 ounces hidden in a box of luxury chocolates. The eggs could be worth a considerable amount of money to dishonest dealers who would sell them to collectors.

'We had no idea what we were carrying. Someone asked us to deliver the box to a relative,' Kathy claimed.

The strange tale began in Oxford where Kathy and Jennifer met a group of wealthy young students at a party. 'This guy called Norman invited us on a luxury holiday on his father's yacht in the Caribbean. Norman fixed us up with visas and tickets but at the last moment said he wouldn't be able to join us until a few days later. It all seemed too good to be true... and it was.'

---

2 Quickly read the article you have not yet looked at.
Which one do you think comes from a 'popular paper' and which one comes from a 'quality paper'?
Which one:

- carries more information?
- is more 'emotional'?
- has more human interest?
- do you find more difficult?

SPEAKING

What kind of person do you think Kathy is?
Do you believe her story?
What effect do you think the stories had on the girls' families?

WRITING

I thought you should know...

Write a letter to two friends who are travelling around the world. Tell them all about Kathy and Jennifer.
Remember to say if you believe their story and what *you* think should happen to them.
Give your friends some advice about accepting gifts from strangers.
Begin the letter like this:

> Dear Megan and Janet,
> I hope you get this letter before you leave Australia. I thought you should know about the two girls who've been arrested for smuggling.

LISTENING

The news

1 Listen and write down the three news headlines.
What will they be about?

2 Now listen to the whole of the news. Were your predictions correct?

3 Listen again to the first news item about changes in the traffic regulations.

When do the new regulations come into force? Which vehicles will they apply to?
What arrangements are being made to make the changeover easier?

4 Listen again to the news item about the fire and fill in the gaps.

A (1) .... at the Local Examinations Board (2) .... a wing of
the building. The (3) .... fire (4) .... at around 3 o'clock this
morning and it took until 9.00 for firemen to bring it (5) .... control.
Fortunately damage (6) .... limited to the Science examinations section.
A (7) .... has said that a (8) .... , I'm sorry I'll read that
again, a hundred (9) .... who took the November (10) ....
will have to re-sit. A group of students is (11) .... police with their
(12) ....

5 Which tenses are used in the first two news items? Can you explain why?

WRITING

Newspaper articles

1 Expand these notes to complete a 'nonsense' news item.

1 Bad weather/cause/destruction/this year's spaghetti crop/Northern Italy.
2 crop/destroy/exceptionally cold weather/this time of year.
3 Farmers/wake up/this morning/find/spaghetti/freeze/branches/their trees.
4 This mean/ruin/thousands/Italian farmers/who/depend/this year's harvest.
5 This be/third year/spaghetti harvest/be disaster.
6 Farmers/must/wonder/if/they/be/rescue/European Community again.

2 Here is another 'nonsense' article to expand.

1 Finally/World Animal Fund/announce/plans/save/penguins/extinction.
2 want/build/electric fence/penguin breeding grounds/Antarctic.
3 believe/only way/prevent/hungry polar bears/eat/ all the penguins.
4 polar bears/eat/bananas instead.
5 Next Monday/group/pop stars/make a record/raise money/the project.

Were the words you used 'information words' or 'grammar words'?

3 In pairs, or small groups, think of a 'nonsense' news item. Write it down and
then choose one person from each group to read it to the rest of the class.

WRITING PREPARATION

Composition writing

1 Read the composition and look at its relationship with the plan on the right.

> Every day popular papers print stories about the private lives of public people. Journalists believe they have the right to invade their privacy; their victims disagree.
>
> After all, isn't what the famous do behind closed doors their own business? A politician's unhappy marriage is unimportant. What matters is how well he does his job.
>
> There again, how he acts in private may show us his true nature. Public figures must also realize that the loss of privacy is the price of fame.
>
> There is no clear answer. Let's hope the journalists and their subjects behave in an honest and decent way.

Popular newspapers - stories, private lives of public people. Journalists/photographers think OK - victims disagree

Private life = own business Good at job = important, not marriage

Private life reflects true nature Fame = loss of privacy

No right answer

2 Now make a plan for this composition.

> Television is one of this century's most important inventions. However, are we its master or its slave?
>
> Some say that it has killed the art of conversation. In other words, people no longer know how to amuse themselves because they are so used to the instant entertainment it provides.
>
> There again, it has brought many benefits. The news keeps us informed of world events, it can educate us and we can even watch a live football match on the other side of the world.
>
> To sum up, it has changed our lives, but it is up to us whether we let it enrich or dominate them.

3 Make a plan for this composition: *Newspapers should be politically independent.*

READING

Look at the cartoons and the captions. Imagine you wanted to explain the jokes to someone who hadn't seen them. What would you say?

The real reason dinosaurs became extinct

Suddenly, Bobby felt very alone in the world.

Disaster befalls Professor Schnabel's cleaning lady when she mistakes his time machine for a new dryer.

VOCABULARY

1 Dictionary definitions

This key vocabulary will help you with the listening and reading in this unit.
Use the words in the box to complete the dictionary definitions. Note the context
and forms in which any of these words appears in this Unit.

| meteor   mammal   dwell   drought   genetics   fossil   reptile   ancestor |

1 .... /ˈreptaɪl/ a rough-skinned creature whose blood
changes temperature according to the temperature around it.
2 .... /dwel/ formal; to live in a place.
3 .... /ˈmiːtjəʳ/ a small piece of matter floating in space that
forms a line of light if it falls into the earth's air.
4 .... /ˈfɒsəl/ a hardened part or print of an animal or plant of
long ago, that has been preserved in rock or ice.
5 .... /draʊt/ a long period of dry weather when there is not enough
water.
6 .... /dʒəˈnetɪks/ a study of how living things develop according
to the effects of those substances passed on in the cell from the parents.
7 .... /ˈmæməl/ an animal of the type which is fed, when young, on
its mother's milk.
8 .... /ˈænsestəʳ/ a person, esp. one living a long time ago, from
whom another is descended.

2 Science and scientists

See if you can complete the names of the sciences and their scientists.

1 Amongst other things, Galileo was an *ast* .... Gazing at the stars is
called *ast* ....
2 Some *anth* .... went into the jungle to study the life of an Indian tribe.
They were never seen again. The science of *anth* .... will miss them!
3 *Geo* .... is a very important science when people are searching for
oil. *Geo* .... take rock samples and analyze them.
4 *Arch* .... is the study of the remains of ancient times. Indiana Jones is
a famous *arch* .... from the cinema!

● Which one of these sciences is the most/the least interesting? Which one do you
think is the most useful?

SPEAKING

Time travellers

A new time machine means that expeditions can be made to: the Age of the
Dinosaurs; the Ice-Age; the Age of Columbus; the year 3000.

1 Discuss which three people you would choose for each expedition: astronomer,
geologist, painter, poet, anthropologist, soldier, nurse, botanist, priest/nun,
astrologer, archaeologist, linguist, explorer.

2 Which expedition would you like to go on? Choose one of the roles. Write a
speech explaining who you are and why you want to go. Read it to the class.

LISTENING
Living dinosaurs

Patricia Osborne has just been to the 'Living Dinosaurs' exhibition with her daughter, Katie. They have just got home to their flat where Pop Osborne is doing some housework.

The listening is in two parts.

1 Part A

Patricia is talking to Pop Osborne.

1 Listen to their conversation and find out:
  • what is special about the exhibition.
  • how suitable it is for children.

2 Listen again and fill in the missing part of the conversation.

POP OSBORNE: Hello Pat. What have you been ....[1]?

PATRICIA: I've just taken Katie to an exhibition.

POP OSBORNE: ....[2], you ....[3].

PATRICIA: Tired! ....[4].

POP OSBORNE: ....[5]. I'll make a nice cup of tea. So, what did you see?

PATRICIA: Well, it was called 'Living Dinosaurs'.

POP OSBORNE: 'Living Dinosaurs'! You ....[6]!

PATRICIA: Of course they were models which look like dinosaurs... They're operated ....[7]. They do all the right things. Move and ....[8] and make horrible ....[9].

POP OSBORNE: Katie ....[10].

PATRICIA: Actually she ....[11] it. One little chap was ....[12]. He ....[13] more than four.

POP OSBORNE: Oh ....[14], ...[15]. He'll probably have ....[16].

2 Sincerely sympathetic! 📼

1 Pop Osborne uses the following expressions to show sympathy.

Listen to the recording and practise saying them aloud, copying Pop Osborne's intonation as closely as you can. In the first one, a line shows what happens to his voice. Do the same for the other examples.

a Poor you!   c Oh dear!
b Never mind!   d What a shame!

2 How could you reply to the following statements? Sometimes more than one answer is possible!

a 'I've got an awful headache!'
  .... I'll get you some aspirin.
b 'I'm sorry, I can't find that book you lent me.'
  .... ! It's not important.
c 'My dog has been run over by a bus!'
  .... ! He was such a nice dog.
d 'I can't do this exercise!'
  .... ! I'll explain it to you.
e 'The last bus left ten minutes ago.'
  .... ! That means we'll have to walk!

3 Part B

Katie is telling Pop what happened to the dinosaurs.

Listen to their conversation and find answers to these questions.
1 When did the dinosaurs die out?
2 Why did they disappear? What did people use to think?
3 What do scientists believe these days?
4 What made them change their minds?
5 Why didn't all the other animals die as well?
6 How long did dinosaurs live on the earth?

LANGUAGE STUDY
Making intelligent guesses

1 Look at these sentences from the recording.

1 You **must be** tired.
2 It **might have been** a change in the weather.
3 Katie **must have been** scared.
4 He **can't have been** more than four.
5 It **could have been** a meteor.
6 You **can't be** serious.

Which sentences are:
- certain, in a positive sense?
- certain, in a negative sense?
- uncertain?
- talking about now/talking about the past?

What happens to their structure when they go from present to past?

2 Stress patterns 🔊
Listen to sentences **1** and **2** again. Notice where the **stress** lies and how the *unstressed* words are pronounced (e.g. 'be' in sentence **1**).

1 *You **must** be **tired**.*
2 *It **might** have been a **change** in the weather.*

Try to copy their pronunciation as closely as you can.

How do you think the other sentences will be pronounced?

3 Complete the text using one of these forms.
For *definitely*, a form based on **must**.
For *definitely not*, a form based on **can't**.
For *possibly*, a form based on **might** or **could**.

Be careful! Some of the sentences use the passive.

There are many strange cases of 'living fossils'. These are creatures which come to life after millions of years when they are freed from inside rocks. The most extraordinary event was in 1856 in northern France, where engineers were making a railway tunnel. They broke open a rock and a big ugly bird, with two legs and a beak full of sharp teeth flew out. It flapped its wings a few times but then died.

They took its body to a museum where an expert said that the bird (1)*definitely be* a pterodactyl. Its form could be seen in the rock where it (2)*definitely trap*. Scientists believed it (3) *possibly fall* into a swamp (an area of soft, wet land). The bird (4)*definitely not die*; instead, it (5)*definitely go* into a kind of coma, like a deep sleep. It (6)*definitely catch* in the swamp at least a hundred and fifty million years ago, before the swamp turned to rock. Some of these prehistoric birds (7)*definitely be* much bigger; some (8)*possibly have* wings which were fifteen metres across. Some people did not believe the engineers' story; they said the creature (9)*definitely not survive* all that time, but I feel they (10)*definitely tell* the truth.

SPEAKING

Mystery cultures

Work in pairs. Each of you is an archaeologist with a different interest.

STUDENT A look at p. 139.
STUDENT B look at p. 143.

READING

'Man After Man'

1 Before you read, think about these questions:
● How much longer will man survive?
● What do you understand by 'genetic engineering'?

2 Read the text and decide if these statements are **true** or **false**.

1 War destroys mankind.
2 In a thousand years, there will be no human beings surviving on Earth.
3 The new species have evolved naturally.
4 One of the new species is able to fly.
5 The Tundra Dweller depends on the creature which lives on the plains.
6 The Tundra Dweller goes through three important stages.
7 The 'newcomers' want to settle on Earth.
8 In the end, only one descendant of man is likely to survive.

3 Word search
Search the text and find the different ways which are used to express the idea of something dying or ending.

SPEAKING

● How likely do you think Dixon's predictions are?
● Make your own prediction of how Man will look in five million years! Will he still be around? How many eyes, legs, arms will he have? How will he communicate/travel/reproduce etc?

We know how mankind has evolved till now, but what is his future? In his fascinating anthropology of the future, *Man After Man*, Dougal Dixon makes some suggestions.

He predicts that, within 200 years, man will have reached crisis point. Overpopulation and industrial pollution will have made life impossible for most of us. Civilization will have broken down and billions of people will starve and die. A few specially chosen human beings will leave Earth on giant spaceships in search of new planets. On Earth, scientists will try two ways of adjusting man to the changing environment. In a first attempt, a tiny number of adapted humans will live on, helped by high technology. But they will become extinct in a thousand years along with the last remaining farmers and fishermen. Man as we would recognize him will no longer exist.

The scientists' second attempt to preserve mankind is more successful: they genetically engineer five new species based around humans. What would normally take three and a half million years, only takes thirty years. One of the new species lives in tropical forest, another can survive in the desert. A third (Piscanthropus profundus) can live and breathe deep in the oceans. The two remaining species are particularly interesting. They are the Tundra Dweller who inhabits the land of the melting ice caps, and the Woodland Dweller.

These two eventually depend on each other because the Tundra Dweller migrates to the woods in winter. At first they are enemies but eventually they rely on one another – the Tundra Dweller carries the Woodland Dweller and provides it with warmth. In return, it depends on the intelligence of its passenger.

They start to die out but, as the Earth becomes hotter, the Tundra Dweller adapts by losing its hair and growing fat. Instead of warmth, its body provides food for the transformed Woodland Dweller.

But nothing lasts for ever. After five million years, descendants of the men who left Earth return in giant spacecraft. They too have evolved and come back to exploit the Earth's resources. All the land creatures suddenly die out except for genetically engineered workers and an ugly food creature: the final form of the Tundra Dweller. Their work complete, the 'newcomers' leave and everything dies. Yet, deep in the oceans there is 'Piscanthropus profundus', which has managed to escape all of these changes. Perhaps this last descendant of man will eventually come out of the sea to evolve into other creatures who will inhabit the land.

LANGUAGE STUDY

Future predictions

A few specially chosen human beings **will leave** Earth on giant spaceships in search of new planets. Civilization **will have broken down**.

- We often use the simple future (**will**) for predictions.
- The 'future perfect' (**will have done**) is used when we predict that, by a point in the future, something has already happened.

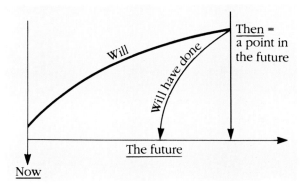

1 *Imagine...*

The year is 2,200. Yonotot Nartrog has just taken off in one of the spacecraft. She has extremely regular habits. She plans to take a food pill three times a day, write a page in her diary once a day, play chess once a week, watch a video every month and drink a bottle of Happy Juice on her birthday! Calculate what she will have done by the year 2,250. Fortunately a new 'Space Year' is 500 days (not 365) and has 50 ten-day weeks! Each space month is five weeks.

2 Make some predictions about your own life. Example: *By the time I'm 30 I'll have...*

LANGUAGE STUDY

Linking, explaining and contrasting

In earlier units we have looked at some of the ways we can join short sentences to make longer sentences, talk about 'cause and effect', give explanations and make contrasts. Choose the words and expressions which can be used to complete the text about the evolution of money. Sometimes, more than one possibility is correct.

It is difficult to imagine a world without money, though of course, it hasn't always been around.

1   **A** *First of all,* **B** *Once upon a time,* **C** *Firstly,* **D** *In the beginning,* people would exchange sheep for ivory, or goats for weapons.
2   **A** *Sincerely,* **B** *Of course,* **C** *Naturally,* this could be inconvenient.
3   An easier way of trading was needed, **A** *so that* **B** *because* **C** *that's why* money had to be invented.
4   **A** *Lately,* **B** *Once,* **C** *Eventually,* four-and-a-half-thousand years ago in Mesopotamia (now Southern Iraq) someone had a brilliant idea.
5   They realized that it would be easier **A** *for* **B** *in order to* **C** *to* buy and sell by using standard weights of silver.
6   This was a marvellous invention because **A** *unless* **B** *otherwise* **C** *instead* we might still be swapping things for sheep and goats!
7   However, it wasn't **A** *before* **B** *by* **C** *until* the seventh century BC that the first coins appeared in the ancient kingdom of Lydia (now Turkey).
8   **A** *During* **B** *By* **C** *Over* the next few centuries, the use of coins spread to other civilized countries.
9   Rulers wanted to control the issue of coins, **A** *because* **B** *so* **C** *so that* **D** *that's why* they were stamped with the head of the ruler and their value.
10 **A** *As* **B** *While* **C** *Because* precious metals like silver and gold were used, they were actually worth the weight of the metal.
11 Chinese copper coins were **A** *so* **B** *too* **C** *very* **D** *really* heavy to carry that people kept them with merchants
12 **A** *which* **B** *whom* **C** *that* **D** *who* gave their customers receipts written on pieces of paper.
13 **A** *After* **B** *Afterwards* **C** — they would use them
14 **A** *like* **B** *as* **C** *for* **D** *instead* money.
15 **A** *Eventually,* **B** *Lastly,* in the fourteenth century, the Chinese government introduced the first paper money.
16 **A** *Because* **B** *Although* **C** *Despite* people were suspicious at first, they accepted it.
17 Nowadays, nobody thinks twice about using paper money, **A** *despite* **B** *although* **C** *while* it only has symbolic rather than intrinsic value. (This is true of coins, too).
18 There is nothing new in this **A** *so* **B** *because* **C** *that's why* **D** *as* tribes have traded for centuries using shells and even feathers as currency.
19 **A** *Nowadays,* **B** *These days,* **C** *Actually,* less and less cash is used and we pay for expensive items like record players and cars by cheque and credit card.
20 **A** *In fact,* **B** *Really,* **C** *Nevertheless,* people predict that, by the end of the century, coins and paper money will have been completely replaced by plastic money.

LISTENING

1 You are going to hear a short talk about the evolution of armour. Before you listen, look at the pictures and see how many of these items you can find.

helmet   breast-plate   sword   chain-mail   spear   shield

2 While you listen, make notes for each picture as the lecturer discusses it. Then compare your notes with a partner and listen to the passage again.

WRITING

From your notes write a composition on the evolution of armour. Use the exercise about the story of money as a guide.

117

Pedigree

SPEAKING | Talking about family relationships

Queen Victoria's descendants have married into most of the royal families of Europe. Study the family tree of the House of Windsor.

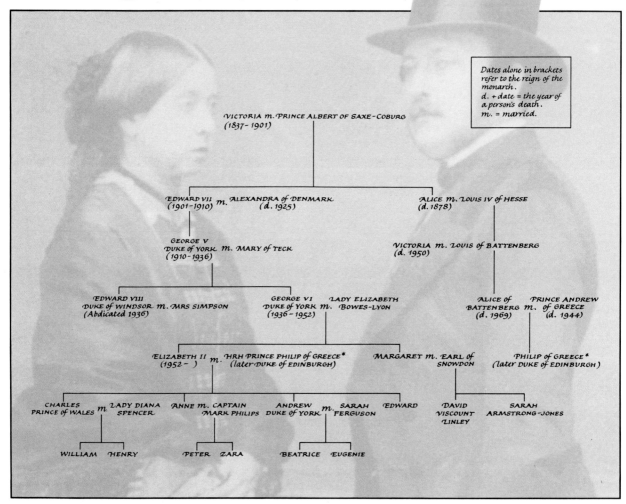

Dates alone in brackets refer to the reign of the monarch.
d. + date = the year of a person's death.
m. = married.

VICTORIA m. PRINCE ALBERT OF SAXE-COBURG
(1837-1901)

EDWARD VII m. ALEXANDRA OF DENMARK
(1901-1910)   (d. 1925)

ALICE m. LOUIS IV OF HESSE
(d. 1878)

GEORGE V
DUKE OF YORK m. MARY OF TECK
(1910-1936)

VICTORIA m. LOUIS OF BATTENBERG
(d. 1950)

EDWARD VIII
DUKE OF WINDSOR m. MRS SIMPSON
(Abdicated 1936)

GEORGE VI   LADY ELIZABETH
DUKE OF YORK m. BOWES-LYON
(1936-1952)

ALICE OF   PRINCE ANDREW
BATTENBERG m. OF GREECE
(d. 1969)   (d. 1944)

ELIZABETH II m. HRH PRINCE PHILIP OF GREECE*
(1952-)   (later DUKE OF EDINBURGH)

MARGARET m. EARL OF
SNOWDON

PHILIP OF GREECE*
(later DUKE OF EDINBURGH)

CHARLES   LADY DIANA   ANNE m. CAPTAIN   ANDREW m. SARAH   EDWARD
PRINCE OF WALES m. SPENCER   MARK PHILIPS   DUKE OF YORK FERGUSON

DAVID   SARAH
VISCOUNT   ARMSTRONG-JONES
LINLEY

WILLIAM   HENRY   PETER   ZARA   BEATRICE   EUGENIE

1 Using the family tree, answer these questions.

1 Who was Queen Elizabeth's mother-in-law?
2 What is the relationship between Queen Elizabeth and:
   ● David Viscount Linley?   ● King Edward VIII of England?
3 Who is Queen Victoria's eldest great-great-great-great-grandson?
4 What is the relationship between Queen Victoria and the Duke of Edinburgh?
5 What is the relationship between Prince Andrew of Greece and Louis of Battenberg?
6 Who are Prince William and Prince Henry's cousins?

2 Vocabulary

Make a list of words to describe family relationships, e.g. *mother*, *cousin*, *uncle*.

3

Do you still have a royal family in your country? If so, is there any connection with the British royal family? Could you extend the family tree shown here?

4

Draw your own family tree. Write sentences to describe your relationship with other family members. In groups of three tell each other about your own families.

READING

Heirs to the throne

1

Read the passage about the royal princes and answer the following questions.

1 Who are second and third in line to the British throne?
2 When is it predicted that William will succeed?
3 What will be special about him?
4 How much Greek, Polish, German, Russian and Danish blood do the princes have?
5 How often has the throne gone to the second child in the House of Windsor?

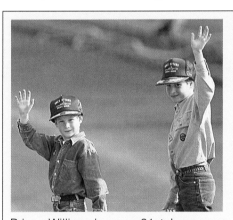

Prince William, born on 21st June 1982, is second in line to the throne, (1) .... his father, Prince Charles. This means that in the normal course of events, he should succeed (2) .... the throne in around 2030. He is likely to be (3) .... most English monarch (4) .... about four hundred years!

He is 39% English, 16% Scottish with 6.25% each (5) .... Irish and American. The rest is an interesting mixture of Greek, Danish, German, Russian and Polish. He gets most of (6) .... through his grandfather Prince Philip, (7) .... is able to trace his family through (8) .... every royal house of Europe.

His younger brother Henry, who was born (9) .... September 1984, is third in line. It is worth remembering (10) ...., in the House (11) .... Windsor, the throne (12) .... often gone to the second child. Edward VII was Queen Victoria's second child (13) .... he succeeded to the throne because the eldest child was a girl. George V became King (14) .... his elder brother died young, and George VI came to (15) .... throne because his brother (16) .... to abdicate so that he (17) .... marry Mrs Simpson. Because of past history, and in case (18) .... accidents, Henry will never be (19) .... to fly in the (20) .... plane as his brother, William.

2

Now fill each of the blanks with one word only.

119

READING | Forbidden love

1 Read the text and make a list of important dates and events.

In 1986 the Duchess of Windsor died in Paris a lonely old woman. Yet fifty years earlier, as Mrs Wallis Simpson, she had been at the centre of the abdication of Edward VIII.

Her father had been a wealthy American businessman but his sudden death meant she was **brought up** in relatively poor circumstances. Her mother remained socially ambitious and Wallis **took after** her. After a failed first marriage Wallis married Ernest Simpson, an Anglo-American who had **come into** a family fortune.

In 1929, they moved to London, where she became a successful high-society hostess. She soon became bored with Ernest, and a firm friendship developed between her and Edward, the heir to the throne.

Out of loyalty to the Royal Family, the British press kept the story a secret and any foreign papers which reported it were kept out of Britain. In December 1935, Edward became King and the final crisis was near. Edward's mother, Queen Mary, **looked down on** Wallis and was completely against any idea of marriage. She and the Prime Minister tried to make Edward end the relationship.

The story finally became public when the Bishop of Bradford publicly denounced the affair. Wallis ran away to France. Public opinion would not let a twice-divorced American woman become Queen. The King would have to choose between Wallis and the throne. On 11th December 1936, he abdicated, and left England for a life of exile with the woman he loved.

On Edward's death in 1972, his body was buried in St George's Chapel, Windsor.

2 Answer the following questions on the text.

1 What do you imagine Wallis's childhood was like?
2 When she went to London, how did Wallis become popular so quickly?
3 Why did so few people know about the relationship between Wallis and Edward?
4 What happened after Edward's abdication?

VOCABULARY | Phrasal verbs in context

1 Four phrasal verbs are highlighted in the text in **bold** type. In the infinitive decide which ones mean:

1 to inherit a characteristic or physical feature from a parent
2 to inherit money or property
3 to consider someone else as inferior to oneself
4 to raise/to educate

2 Write a sentence of your own for each of the phrasal verbs.

3 Word search
Go through the text and make a list of any words to do with royalty.

SPEAKING

Evaluating the text

1 What would you have done in Edward's place?
2 Do you feel sorry for anyone in the story?
3 Who do you feel was responsible for his abdication? Put these people in order of their 'guilt': the Bishop, Wallis, the press, Queen Mary, Edward, Wallis's mother, the Prime Minister.

WRITING

Imagine you are one of the principal characters and write a 100-word paragraph giving your point of view about what happened.

LANGUAGE STUDY

Make and **let**

1 Study these two sentences which show how **make** and **let** are used.

1 *She and the Prime Minister tried to* **make** *Edward end the relationship.*
Here **make** means **oblige** or **force**.
2 *Public opinion would not* **let** *a twice-divorced American woman become Queen.*
Here **let** means **allow**.

2 Using the word in brackets, continue the sentences so that they have the same sense as the ones above.

1 Brothers and sisters in ancient Egyptian and Inca royal families could marry each other.
Brothers and sisters in ancient Egyptian and Inca royal families ....
.... (allow)
2 In some societies men can have more than one wife.
Some societies .... (let)
3 She had to marry him even though she didn't love him.
Her parents .... (make)
4 Child marriages are allowed in gypsy communities.
Gypsy communities .... (let)
5 In the Tallensi culture of Ghana, young men are obliged to look for wives outside their tribe.
Tallensi tribes .... (make)
6 The prince's parents wouldn't let him marry the actress.
The prince .... (allow)

SPEAKING

Marriage customs

In some parts of Southern Germany, the bride receives a loaf of bread and the bridegroom a glass of beer. Then, together, they saw a log in half. What do you think this custom means?
Work in groups. Write your answers on separate pieces of paper and then compare them. Did any two in the group have the same answer?

LANGUAGE STUDY

Time expressions

Decide which of the two words in brackets best completes the following sentences.

1 Queen Victoria reigned (for/during) 64 years.
2 The Prime Minister changed 27 times (for/during) Victoria's reign.
3 (While/Meanwhile,) she ruled her empire, her heir, Edward, was preparing to become King.
4 (While/Meanwhile,) he gained a reputation as a playboy.
5 Edward VII (lately/eventually) became King on her death in 1900.
6 Film of his coronation has (lately/eventually) been discovered in an attic.
7 He died in 1910 (after/afterwards) a short but popular reign.
8 (After/Afterwards,) his son became George V.
9 Wallis had already been married (before/previously) she met the heir to the throne.
10 She had (before/previously) been married to a pilot.

WRITING

Writing a story from notes

Study these notes and then write the story of Juan Carlos and Sofia's royal romance. Decide which information you will/won't include. Try to use some of the time expressions from the previous exercise.

1931 Alfonso XIII leaves Spain for exile in France.
1938 Juan Carlos, his grandson, is born in Rome. Princess Sofia is born in Athens.
1941 –46 Juan Carlos's family takes refuge in Switzerland. Princess Sofia goes into exile.
1946 Sofia returns to Greece.
1948 Juan Carlos goes to Spain to continue his education.
1954 Sofia's mother, Queen Federika, arranges a cruise on her yacht for the young royals of Europe. Sofia and Juan Carlos meet for the first time.
1958 Juan Carlos and Sofia meet again at a wedding in Stuttgart.
1960 They meet at the Sailing Olympics in Naples.
1961 They sit together at a wedding reception in England. They start to go out with each other. In September, they announce their engagement.
1962 They get married on May 14th.
1963 Their first child, Elena, is born.
1965 A second daughter, Cristina, is born.
1968 A son, Felipe, is born.
1969 General Franco announces that Juan Carlos will succeed him as head of state.
1975 Franco dies. Juan Carlos becomes King of Spain.

LANGUAGE STUDY

Subject·object questions

Not all love stories end happily. Look at this summary from a programme of the play *Romeo and Juliet* by William Shakespeare.

1 Read it through quickly and find out how many characters are mentioned and how many deaths are involved.

The Montagues and Capulets are the two most important families in Verona but hate each other. Romeo, Lord Montague's son, and Juliet, Capulet's daughter, meet by chance at a feast and fall in love. The next day Friar Laurence marries them in secret. Following an argument about Romeo's presence at the feast, Tybalt, a member of the Capulet family, murders Romeo's friend Mercutio. Romeo takes his revenge and kills Tybalt. Prince Escalus banishes Romeo from Verona. Capulet, who knows nothing of the secret marriage, tries to make Juliet marry Prince Paris. Juliet wants to escape this marriage. Friar Laurence gives her a drug to make her appear dead but Romeo does not hear about the trick. He returns to Verona and kills Prince Paris, whom he blames for Juliet's death. He drinks some poison by Juliet's side and dies. When she awakes, she realizes what has happened and kills herself with a dagger.

2 Look at these questions and answers.

Who loves Romeo?   → Juliet. Juliet does.
SUBJECT OBJECT

Who does Romeo love?   → Juliet. He loves Juliet.
OBJECT SUBJECT

So, when **who** or **what** is the SUBJECT of a question, we don't use the auxilliary **do/did**.

3 Using the prompts on the left, make questions for the answers on the right.

1 Where/the lovers/meet?   → At a feast.
2 Who/marry them?   → Friar Laurence.
3 Who/kill/Mercutio?   → Tybalt.
4 What/Romeo/do   → He kills Tybalt to avenge Mercutio.
5 What/happen/Romeo   → He is banished from Verona.
6 What/make/Juliet/appear dead? → A drug Friar Laurence gives her.
7 Who/Romeo/kill?   → Prince Paris.
8 Why/Romeo/kill/him?   → Because he blames him for Juliet's death.
9 What/kill/Romeo?   → The poison he drinks.
10 What/happen/Juliet/wake up? → She sees Romeo's body and kills herself.

LISTENING | Henry VIII and his six wives

1 Henry VIII (reign 1509–1547) had six wives. Listen to the interview and complete the table.

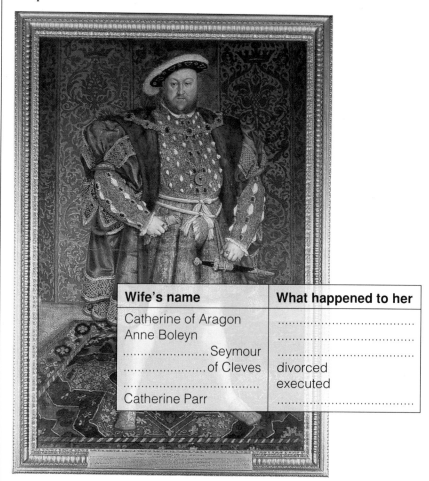

Wife's name	What happened to her
Catherine of Aragon	....
Anne Boleyn	....
........................Seymour	....
........................of Cleves	divorced
....	executed
Catherine Parr	....

2 Listen again and answer these more detailed questions.

1 What else is Henry famous for?
2 Why did he marry so often?
3 Why did Henry form the Church of England?
4 How did Cromwell help Henry?
5 Why did Cromwell lose his head?

3 Look at the tapescript on p. 158.
a Which ways are used to express obligation.
b Which phrasal verbs mean:
   (i) to continue? (ii) to hate/consider someone as inferior
   (iii) to attack (iv) to maintain.

4 Tell each other about a 'larger than life' figure from your country's history.

READING

The best job in the world?

Imagine that you are the Editor of a magazine for young people. One of your journalists has given you this article to be included in the next edition.

1 Read the text and see if there is anything in it that you find surprising or amusing. What is the balance between the light and humorous, and the more serious elements?

Have you ever day-dreamed and wondered what it would be like to be the Queen? Just for fun, let's treat it like any ordinary job and weigh up its good and bad points.

To begin with, the money's not bad. She gets a 'salary' of four million pounds a year from the British government. There is no tax on any of her income and, when she dies, her heirs won't have to pay a penny. What's more, she doesn't have to put stamps on letters: the royal seal is enough. She also uses special black blotting paper to dry the ink on letters. (It has to be black so nobody can read any state secrets from it!)

Then, of course, there's the power and the foreign travel. She can declare war, dismiss the government and pardon everybody in prison!

It is the perfect job if you like going abroad. The Queen travels all round the world in style, visiting fascinating places. There are some great presents as well: on two of her trips she was given a crocodile and two hippos.

Now let's look at the minuses. There are lots of boring, formal dinners to attend (bad news if you've got a weight problem) and speeches to give. She always has to be diplomatic and isn't allowed to speak her mind. It must also be hard knowing who your real friends are and who are just 'yes men'.

Possibly the worst thing is the lack of privacy. True, on the one hand she has lots of homes where she can hide away, but on the other hand, there are always photographers trying to take pictures of her whatever she is doing. It must be very difficult trying to keep a balance between public life and a private family life.

While I wouldn't mind the money, it must be a minor consideration for such a rich woman. I'm sure there is part of her which would rather live in peace and quiet, enjoying her wealth. Fortunately for the British people, the Royal Family's tradition of service means we have a monarch prepared to bear the heavy responsibility of the Crown. I wouldn't want the job.

2 Make a list of all the points the writer makes and decide if they are important (I) of secondary importance (SI), or light and humorous (LH).

Example: *advantages: £4 million a year* (I), *no stamps* (SI), *black blotting paper* (LH)

3 Understanding the organization of the text

Search the text for ways that the writer: orders points, gives opinions, balances arguments and draws conclusions.

4 Writing

Your magazine has just been given a big advertisement. In order to make room for it, you have to cut the article about the Queen by 50%. How will you do it? Look at your list of points and decide which points you will cut. (A lot will depend on how serious you want to make your article.)
Show your teacher your list of points and then write the shorter version.

SPEAKING
Spitting images?

Here are several pictures of the British Royal Family. One is real; some are photographs of puppets which are used in a satirical TV comedy programme.

1 Match each satirical photograph with a standard one of the same person.

2 What do you think of these photographs? Are they funny/fair/cruel?

LISTENING

The British Royal Family

You are going to hear four passers-by giving their points of view about the Royal Family.

1 Listen once and look at the photographs. Decide who said what. Then listen a second time and make a list of the points made by the people being interviewed.
Decide whether they are positive, negative or neutral.

2 Leading questions
Listen to these ways of asking someone's opinion and try to mark their stress and intonation.

Example: **What do you think of** the Royal Family?

1 **Could you tell me what you think** of the Royal Family?
2 **Do you think** the Royal Family does a good job?
3 **Would you mind telling me** what you think of the Royal Family?

3 Using the types of question used by the interviewer, find out the opinions of some of your classmates.

4 Linking words in connected speech
Listen, and then read this extract from the tapescript. Notice where the stress lies and how words link up (⌒) in connected speech.

It's **not** like⌒in the⌒**old**⌒days when the **King led** his⌒**armies**⌒into **battle**.

Now listen to this extract and mark the stress and links in the same way.

Me, I'm unemployed and I have to live off £50 a week but they've got millions.

WRITING

Balancing arguments

You are going to write a follow-up magazine article called: 'What ordinary people think about royalty'.

1 In pairs or groups, compare the lists of points you made in the listening exercise. Decide on four positive and four negative points you are going to use in your articles.

2 Now describe your own opinions and what your conclusion will be. Make notes, and plan your article. When your plan is ready, show it to your teacher.

3 Now write the article. This introductory paragraph will help you to get started.

What do ordinary people think about royalty? Does it still have a role in this day and age or should it be abolished? We decided to go out on the streets and find out from ordinary men and women what they thought of royalty and its future.

UNIT 15 | *After Dark*

READING

1 Read the text.
What is the connection between the ghostly piper and the castle in the picture below?

There is a terrible tale associated with this Scottish castle. In the seventeenth century it belonged to **1 A** *one* **B** *– 0* **C** *the* Campbell family, **2 A** *their* **B** *whose* **C** *which* deadliest enemy was 'Left-Handed Coll Macdonnel'. Macdonnel wanted to find a way of killing his enemies, **3 A** *whom* **B** *they* **C** *who* were safely behind the castle's walls, **4 A** *as* **B** *because* **C** *so* he sent his piper to spy on it.

The piper disguised himself and **5 A** *being* **B** *had been* **C** *was* welcomed by the Campbells, **6 A** *what* **B** *whom* **C** *which* he entertained. Unfortunately for him, the Campbells became suspicious and locked him in a tower. The piper had to warn his friends **7 A** *outside* **B** *underneath* **C** *away* that the Campbells were prepared for an attack so he played a famous tune now known **8 A** *about* **B** *of* **C** *as* 'The Piper's warning to his Master'. Macdonnel understood **9 A** *that* **B** *what* **C** *which* had happened and turned **10 A** *out* **B** *off* **C** *back*.

The Campbells were so furious **11 A** *so* **B** *because* **C** *that* they cut off the piper's hands and the brave man died. **12 A** *When* **B** *While* **C** *After* the castle's present owners **13 A** *have* **B** *have had* **C** *had* it restored, workmen discovered a handless skeleton under the cellar floor. His spirit **14 A** *yet* **B** *still* **C** *always* lives on in the castle, **15 A** *when* **B** *where* **C** *which* even today you can sometimes hear him playing.

2 Read the text again and, for each number, decide which of the three choices, **A**, **B** or **C**, is correct.

3 Discussion
- What do you think of the story?
- Was the piper brave?
- Do you think he really does haunt the castle?

Do you know a place with a history like this? Tell your classmates the story.

VOCABULARY

Common sounds 📼

These words all describe common sounds. Study the definitions of the sounds and write down the order in which the sounds appear on the recording.

a **bark** /bɑːk/ the sound that dogs make.
b **slam** /slæm/ to shut loudly, with force.
c **gasp** /gɑːsp/ to catch one's breath suddenly because of a shock.
d **rattle** /ˈrætl̩/ to make a lot of quick metallic noises.
e **scream** /skriːm/ to cry out loudly on a high note.
f **snore** /snɔː/ to breathe noisily through the nose and mouth while asleep.
g **squeak** /skwiːk/ a very high but not loud sound.
h **tap** /tæp/ to strike lightly against something.
i **yawn** /jɔːn/ to open the mouth wide and breathe in and out, as when tired.

WRITING

A night to remember

1 You are going to hear a story made up of different sounds and then write it. Before you listen to the sounds, look at the picture and answer the questions. This will help you develop the background.

- When and where was the house built? What kind of history do you think it has?
- Who are the people? How do they feel?
- How would you describe the figure in the doorway? Use your imagination!

2 Listen to the sounds, make notes and plan your story. Then write the story in the PAST. If you need to remind yourselves about narrative tenses, look at p. 32.

READING | Haunted houses

1 Here are two different stories about houses with mysterious problems. The paragraphs are mixed up and in the wrong order. Read the paragraphs and reconstruct the two stories. Paragraph **A** is the beginning of one of the stories. Which story does the picture illustrate?

A Most doctors and scientists refuse to believe in ghosts and psychic happenings. Yet in the 1950's in Yorkshire, in the north of England, two doctors almost changed their minds. A house which they used as their surgery started to make strange noises.

B Almost immediately the husband changed from a hard-working, stable individual to lazy and bad-tempered. Kathleen felt that she was being controlled by something outside her power.

C As the foundations of the house settled, the rest of the house moved too. As final proof, the bangs and noises were at their worst at high tide.

D On a November morning in 1974, one of the sons of the De Feo family took a rifle and murdered the other six members of his family. For the next thirteen months the house in Amityville in the USA stood empty.

E In the garden they discovered an old disused sewer which was connected with a nearby river. It turned out that, at high tide, river water forced its way up the sewer and was making the earth under the house wet and unstable.

F The 'ghostbusters' noticed that the walls of the surgery were cracked and that the roof needed repairing where it dipped in the middle. This suggested that the house had problems with its foundations, so the team decided to investigate.

G None of the local people wished to buy it and the newspapers were full of stories of demonic possession. Eventually, a young couple called George and Kathleen Lutz, believing they had found a bargain because of some ridiculous stories, moved in.

H Things got worse. Their children started to get hurt around the house, and Kathleen Lutz had terrible nightmares about the De Feo family. The couple had the horrible feeling that history was about to repeat itself. Just after the Christmas period, unable to stand it any longer they fled.

I These included loud explosions and the sound of banging, which even made the walls shake. The doctors called in a plumber, who looked over the water pipes, and they had the gas and electrical systems examined. Nobody was able to find out the cause of the noises. By now, the doctors were seriously wondering whether their surgery was haunted and they called in some psychic researchers to investigate.

J Over the next few weeks, thousands of flies appeared in the bedrooms; windows and doors opened and closed for no reason; the toilet bowls turned black and a statue moved around their home on its own. The house was either boiling hot or freezing cold, and they could do nothing to change the temperature.

2 What helped you to put the stories together?

SPEAKING

Discussing the stories

The first story has a logical explanation but the second one seems to accept the explanation of 'demonic' possession. Can you think of logical explanations for what happened when the Lutz family moved into their new home?

LANGUAGE STUDY

Have something done and **need**

1 Look at these two sentences.

a *They had the gas and electrical systems examined.*
b *They examined the gas and electrical systems.*

Which sentence means:
● someone did it for them?
● they did it themselves?

The first sentence uses the construction 'have something done'.

*She **had** her picture **taken** (by a professional photographer).*
Have + something + PAST PARTICIPLE

2 In the text it says:
The roof needed repairing.
Something + need + VERB + -ing

We can re-phrase this without changing its meaning by saying:
The roof needed to be repaired.
Something + need to be + PAST PARTICIPLE

3 Imagine that the surgery has been repaired by workmen. The doctors are now showing a friend around the house and garden. Re-phrase these sentences using one of the forms we have just looked at.

1 Some workmen repaired the roof.
  We ....
2 The wall still needs fixing.
  The wall needs to ....
3 We had the hall re-decorated.
  A painter ....
4 A plumber fixed the pipes and the central heating.
  We ....
5 A builder filled in the old sewer.
  We ....
6 We are going to have the garden dug.
  The garden needs ....

VOCABULARY

All around the house

Martina is a university student studying away from home.
Look at the picture of her room and label it with the words in the box.

| cooker | fireplace | wallpaper | desk | bookcase | sofa |
| basin | bed | rug | radiator | wardrobe | chest of drawers |

WRITING

A room of my own

1 Read Martina's letter and compare it with the picture. What has she forgotten to mention? What changes would you make to it?

Dear Mum and Dad,
    I thought I'd write and tell you about where I'm living. I've got an attic room in a large old house which has been turned into flats. The landlord lives on the ground floor, he seems o.k.
    The room is a bit small but it's cosy. There's a nice big sofa by the radiator and a lovely old fireplace with a mirror above it. My desk is right next to a big bookcase where I've got all my books - so they're all within

easy reach when I'm working! There's a little basin where I can have a wash and a tiny cooker for simple meals and making tea. The bathroom and toilet are just down the corridor. The wallpaper is horrid but I've put some posters up.
    Anyway, I must go-I've got a lecture in half an hour.
        Love,
        Martina.

— wallpaper!

2 Using her letter as a guide, write to a friend describing your favourite room.

WRITING

The story of Princess Elizabeth Balthory

Elizabeth Balthory was one of history's most beautiful and terrible people. She was born in 1560 in Hungary and was related to the King of Poland and the Dracula family.

Finish the story. Expand the notes and put the verbs into their correct forms.

1 When/she be fifteen/she marry/famous count/who be/ Hungary's greatest general/who be often away.
2 At/age/twenty-five/her beauty start/disappear.
3 She believe/she can stay beautiful/have baths/blood/young girls!
4 She send servants/find young women/who be promised/good jobs.
5 Once they reach/castle/they/be thrown/deep dungeons.
6 The girls' blood/be drained/for/countess' bath.
7 After five hundred girls disappear,/the King/hear/rumours.
8 When he/have/castle/search/many terrible things/be found.
9 Because/her noble position/she not be executed/but she be/sealed/small room/until she die.
10 Nowadays,/dark nights,/you can hear/screams/countess and her victims/near ruins/castle!

LISTENING

What a bargain!

Miranda Short is visiting a house with Liz Balfour, an estate agent.

1 Listen and make notes on the good things and bad things about the house.

● What are Miranda and Liz like?
● Would you live in this house?

2 **Checking and confirming**
Study these two sentences from the tape and listen to how they are said.

a It's really big, isn't it?
b They only stayed six weeks, didn't they?

Which one is a real question?
Which one is just checking?
How do you know?

Estate
Agent
E. Balfour

3 Listen to these sentences from the recording and decide which ones are real questions and which ones are just checking.

1 It's been empty for quite a while, hasn't it?
2 You don't believe that, do you?
3 But there had been a murder, hadn't there?

Listen again and practise saying the sentences.

4 Turn to the tapescript on p. 158 and read the dialogue in pairs.

READING

The late arrival

Read the text and answer these questions.

1 Who was 'the late arrival'?
2 What happened to the storyteller?
3 Which of the three pictures below fits the description of 'the late arrival'?

We decided to hold a 'horror' fancy dress party before we had our flat decorated. There were mummies, monsters and people dressed up as Frankenstein. Everyone was making lots of noise and having fun. I had a headache, so I went to my room …

While I was sleeping, I heard a sound at the window so I got up. When I pulled back the curtains, I almost fainted. Outside, there was a woman dressed all in black. I was so surprised, I cried out. I'll never know how she got there because we live on the top floor.

Then, somehow, she managed to come through the window which had been stuck for years. If it hadn't been a fancy dress party, I would have been terrified. As it was, I was scared.

She lifted her hood … she was bald and her skin was smooth and as white as paper. Then she looked at me. She had the strangest eyes I'd ever seen. They were bright green with red pupils! Although I was shocked, I felt attracted by her.

'Where did you get those contact lenses?', I asked.

'That's my little secret,' she whispered, 'but unless you come closer, you won't see my teeth.'

I can't remember what happened next. Since that night, I've felt awful. And these marks on my neck, they won't go away. What on earth's wrong with me, do you think?

LANGUAGE
STUDY

Revision of key language

1 Continue the second sentence in each case so that it means the same as the one above.

1 I went to my room because I had a headache.
I had ....

2 When I heard a sound, I was sleeping.
While ....

3 It was such a surprise, that I cried out.
I ....

4 She succeeded in coming through the window.
She managed ....

5 It was a fancy dress party. I wasn't terrified.
If ....

6 I'd never seen such strange eyes.
She had the ....

7 Despite being shocked, I was attracted to her.
Although ....

8 Come closer, otherwise you won't see my teeth.
Unless ....

9 I've forgotten what happened next.
I can't ....

2 Now check your answers by looking through the text about 'the late arrival'.

LISTENING

Vampire rumours

You are going to listen to an interview in which a boy and a vampire are discussing some of the myths and rumours concerning the powers of vampires and the dangers they face.

Decide whether each rumour is **true** or **false**.

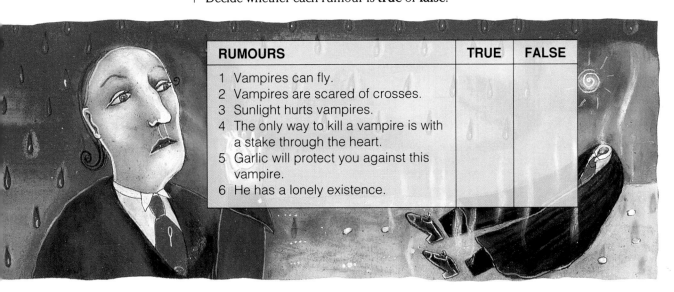

RUMOURS	TRUE	FALSE
1 Vampires can fly.		
2 Vampires are scared of crosses.		
3 Sunlight hurts vampires.		
4 The only way to kill a vampire is with a stake through the heart.		
5 Garlic will protect you against this vampire.		
6 He has a lonely existence.		

Pairwork

VOCABULARY

UNIT 1 ■ SET A ■ PAGE 6

Clothes and fashion

Using the words in the exercise, label dummy 2's clothes. Tell Student B what it is wearing and he/she draws the clothes on his/her dummy 2. Then 'dress' your dummy 1 following Student B's instructions.

UNIT 2 ■ SET C ■ PAGE 21

SPEAKING

An interview with Chris Caine

You are Chris Caine. You are going to be interviewed for *Mondo Movie* magazine. Here are some personal details.

You are fifty-five years old (you say you're forty!) You were born in a poor part of London. Life was hard and you had a poor but happy childhood.

You started your show business career as a singer in a London club. You went to drama school and acted in many plays. You were always so nervous that you were sick before going on stage. This is a long time in the past now!

In 1963, you went to Hollywood and had very small parts in films. Life was hard at first and you slept in your car in car parks. In the first two years you had six accidents because in England everybody drives on the left. You were very homesick and missed your family. Your big opportunity came in 1965 when you played an eccentric English teacher in *Here Comes Lulu*. Since then, you have made thirty films and millions of dollars.

You are now happy in the US and have changed your nationality. You still hate hamburgers though! You have been married three times. (Invent your story!) Now you live alone with six dogs.

UNIT 3 ■ SET D ■ PAGE 31

SPEAKING

Booking a hotel

You are the receptionist at the Avonbury Hotel. It is a two-star hotel five minutes' walk from the station. It is a ten-minute bus ride to the centre of town.

You are busy next week because of the music festival and only have a few rooms left. Here are details of the rooms that are still free.

Room	Mon	Tues	Wed	Thurs	Fri
322 Single room with bath	×	....	×	×	....
441 Single room with shower	×	....	×	....	....
201 Double room with shower	×	×	....	....	×
303 Double room with bath	×	....	....	....	×

Double rooms are £50 per night; single rooms are £30. All prices include breakfast.

UNIT 4 ■ SET C ■ PAGE 39

WRITING

The Vikings are coming!

Study the pictures carefully and describe them to Student B.

UNIT 5 ■ SET B ■ PAGE 46

SPEAKING

Giving advice

> You don't have regular meals, you love chocolate and sweets, never take any exercise and only sleep four hours a night.
> You feel unhappy and want to ask your friend, (Student B), for advice.

UNIT 6 ■ SET B ■ PAGE 55

SPEAKING

Describing a painting

Describe your painting to Student B, who should try to draw it.

UNIT 11 ■ SET A ■ PAGE 95

SPEAKING

The newest continent

You are going to complete a map of the main sights of Australia. The underlined information is the same on your map and Student B's map, but the other information is different. Complete your map by exchanging information with Student B. Do NOT show your map to him/her.

UNIT 12 ▪ SET A ▪ PAGE 103

SPEAKING

Getting the facts straight

You are Kit Lucas, an international reporter with the *Daily Planet*. You are in Zblinkski, the capital of Moronia. You are calling your editor in London with a big story. You spoke to him/her yesterday but the line was bad and the situation has changed. Your editor will tell you the details he/she has. Correct him/her where necessary.

YESTERDAY MORNING AT 6 P.M., THE PRESIDENT OF MORONIA WAS ASSASSINATED BY A BOMB IN A BOX OF CHOCOLATES. A REVOLUTION HAS BEGUN, LED BY THE GREEN SHIRTS. THEY HAVE CAPTURED THE POST OFFICE, THE BRITISH EMBASSY AND THE AIRPORT. 50 PEOPLE HAVE BEEN KILLED AND THIRTEEN MINISTERS HAVE BEEN ARRESTED. THE ARCHBISHOP OF ZBLINKSKI SUPPORTS THE GREEN SHIRTS. IN GROZNY, SOUTH OF ZBLINKSKI, THE ARMY IS SUPPORTING THE REVOLUTION. YOU ARE GOING THERE BY PLANE TOMORROW MORNING. YOU CAN'T SEND MANY PHOTOGRAPHS BECAUSE THE POLICE HAVE ARRESTED YOUR PHOTOGRAPHER.

UNIT 13 ▪ SET C ▪ PAGE 114

SPEAKING

Mystery cultures

You have found these objects. What culture do you think they belong to? Show the pictures to Student B and tell him/her what you think.

Pairwork

UNIT 1 ■ SET A ■ PAGE 6

VOCABULARY

Clothes and fashion

Using the words in the exercise, label dummy 1's clothes. Then listen to Student A's instructions and draw the clothes on your dummy 2. Finally, describe your dummy 1 to Student A and let him/her 'dress' his/her dummy 1.

UNIT 2 ■ SET C ■ PAGE 21

SPEAKING

An interview with Chris Caine

You are a journalist from *Mondo Movie* magazine. You want to find out as much as you can about Chris Caine so you can write an article for your readers.

Find out about:

- background
- early career
- number of films made
- first big opportunity
- unhappy marriages
- reputation as a bad driver
- reputation for being nervous before acting

UNIT 3 ◾ SET D ◾ PAGE 31

SPEAKING

Booking a hotel

You and a friend want to spend three days next week at the Avonbury music festival. A friend has given you the number of the Avonbury Hotel. You want to find out where it is and how far it is from the festival. You would rather have single rooms but don't mind sharing if necessary.

UNIT 4 ◾ SET C ◾ PAGE 39

WRITING

The Vikings are coming!

Study the pictures carefully and describe them to Student A.

UNIT 5 ◾ SET B ◾ PAGE 46

SPEAKING

Giving advice

You are Student A's friend and are worried about his/her lifestyle.
Find out how she/he is and what problems she/he has. Talk about his/her habits and lifestyle and give advice. Think of these topics: eating habits, exercise, sleep, luxuries and spending.

SPEAKING

UNIT 6 ■ SET B ■ PAGE 55

Describing a painting

Describe your painting to Student A, who should try to draw it.

UNIT 11 ■ SET A ■ PAGE 95

SPEAKING

The newest continent

You are going to complete a map of the main sights of Australia. The underlined information is the same on your map and Student A's map, but the other information is different. Complete your map by exchanging information with Student A. Do NOT show your map to him/her.

UNIT 12 ▪ SET A ▪ PAGE 103

SPEAKING

Getting the facts straight

You are the Editor of the *Daily Planet*. You are phoning your correspondent, Kit Lucas, who is covering the events in Moronia. You want to check the story you received yesterday. Tell Kit what you know and he/she will correct you or add extra information where necessary.

THE PRESIDENT'S WIFE HAS BEEN KILLED. ATE A POISONED CHOCOLATE. A REVOLUTION HAS BEGUN. ORGANIZED BY THE GREEN SKIRTS. THEY HAVE CAPTURED THE POST OFFICE AND THE BRITISH SCHOOL. 15 PEOPLE HAVE BEEN KILLED AND 30 MINISTERS HAVE BEEN SHOT. THE BISHOP OF ZBLINKSKI SUPPORTS THE GOVERNMENT. IN GROZNY, NORTH OF ZBLINKSKI, THE ARMY IS SUPPORTING THE REVOLUTION. KIT IS GOING THERE BY TRAIN TOMORROW MORNING BUT CAN'T SEND ANY PHOTOGRAPHS BECAUSE THE ARMY HAS ARRESTED THE PHOTOGRAPHER.

UNIT 13 ▪ SET C ▪ PAGE 114

SPEAKING

Mystery cultures

You have found these objects. What culture do you think they belong to? Show the pictures to Student A and tell him/her what you think.

Irregular Verbs

Here are some of the most common irregular verbs in English.
Add the missing form to complete each 'set'. The first 'set' has been done for you.

INFINITIVE	PAST SIMPLE	PAST PARTICIPLE
be	was/were	been
become	....	become
begin	began	....
....	broke	broken
bring	....	brought
build	built	....
buy	....	bought
....	caught	caught
choose	chose	....
come	came	....
cost	....	cost
do	....	done
drink	drank	....
drive	....	driven
....	ate	eaten
fall	....	fallen
feel	....	felt
fight	fought	....
find	....	found
fly	flew	....
forget	forgot	....
get	got	....
give	....	given
go	went	....
....	had	had
hear	....	heard
hide	hid	....
hold	....	held
....	hurt	hurt
keep	....	kept
know	knew	....

INFINITIVE	PAST SIMPLE	PAST PARTICIPLE
lead	....	led
leave	....	left
let	let	....
lose	....	lost
make	made	....
....	met	met
pay	....	paid
put	put	....
read	....	read
....	rang	rung
run	....	run
say	....	said
see	saw	....
sell	sold	....
sing	....	sung
sit	sat	....
sleep	....	slept
speak	spoke	....
spend	....	spent
stand	stood	....
steal	stole	....
swim	....	swum
take	took	....
teach	....	taught
....	thought	thought
wear	....	worn
....	won	won
write	wrote	....

Prepositions

Revise the prepositions you know by completing the text. Study the pictures and select one of the prepositions from the box.

| towards | onto | out of | in | across | onto | over |
| underneath | between | around | into | through | among |

Before he became a film star, Sid the snake worked in the circus with Fred the snake charmer.

Most of the time he lived 1 .... a basket which was 2 .... Fred's bed.

In the evenings Fred took Sid 3 .... the ring and their act began.

Fred started to play his flute and Sid would rise 4 .... the basket and dance around for a bit.

Then he climbed 5 .... the edge and down 6 .... the floor.

When Fred clapped his hands Sid jumped 7 .... a burning hoop.

After that he wriggled 8 .... some burning coals and 9 .... a pair of extremely sharp knives!

The last part of the act was when Sid pretended to escape! He went slowly 10 .... the audience and everybody started to scream.

They screamed even louder when he went 11 .... them.

The last thing Sid did was to curl 12 .... the neck of the most beautiful girl.

She always screamed the loudest and fell 13 .... the floor.

Life was quite dangerous for Sid, but as we can see it was lots of fun too!

Phrasal Verbs

Here are the twenty-five most important phrasal verbs which appear in *Think Ahead to First Certificate*

1 Match the phrasal verbs on the left with their equivalent on the right. The unit in which they appear is given (e.g. U1)

1 find out U1	**a** care for
2 get on with U1	**b** criticize
3 take on U1	**c** find by chance
4 look for U1	**d** despise
5 give away U1	**e** discover information
6 turn up U3	**f** reduce
7 set off U3	**g** arrive
8 run out U3	**h** invent
9 hold on U3	**i** tell a secret
10 put through U3	**j** inherit – money/property
11 come across U4	**k** begin something new
12 make out U4	**l** wait – on the telephone
13 look after U5	**m** have a (good) relationship
14 give up U5	**n** do something – usually wrong!
15 cut down U5	**o** finish/consume
16 take up U5	**p** connect – on the telephone
17 get over U5	**q** employ
18 make up U6	**r** leave on a journey
19 come up with U6	**s** raise/educate
20 tell off U7	**t** search
21 be up to U7	**u** inherit – characteristic
22 look down on U14	**v** stop
23 bring up U14	**w** recover
24 take after U14	**x** think of a solution
25 come into U14	**y** see with difficulty

2 There are four types of phrasal verb.

Type 1: intransitive e.g. *come to* (recover consciousness)
   These don't take an object.
Type 2: transitive inseparable e.g. *look into* (investigate)
   These must take an object which always comes after the verb.
Type 3: transitive separable e.g. *put off* (postpone)
   The object can either come between the verb and the particle or after the verb. If we use a pronoun then it must go between.
Type 4: three-part. e.g. *put up with* (endure)
   These are always transitive inseparable.

Using the unit references and your dictionaries find out which of the categories the phrasal verbs above fall into. Write the type after each of the phrasal verbs in the list.

3 Use each of the phrasal verbs once only to complete the following sentences which provide a context.

1 She .... such an incredible story nobody would believe her.
2 They .... some valuable paintings in their grandmother's attic.
3 He .... a fortune on his father's death.
4 Have you seen my glasses? I've .... them everywhere but I still can't find them.
5 When we .... the terrible news it really ruined our holiday.
6 Even though I've completely .... chocolate, potatoes and beer I still can't lose weight.
7 She loves cooking. She .... her mother who is an excellent cook.
8 I had to .... your son again for being naughty in class.
9 Oh no! What was he .... this time?
10 When we .... it was so early there were hardly any other cars on the road.
11 On the death of his parents in a plane crash, he was .... by his grandmother.
12 I had to leave my old job because I just couldn't .... my boss.
13 Could you .... my suitcase for five minutes while I make a phone call?
14 I can't .... what this says, it's so old the writing has almost disappeared.
15 You want to speak to Maria? .... I'll check if she's here.
16 After his heart attack he .... yoga to help him relax.
17 There is just too much work; we need to .... an extra person.
18 By the time they .... all the tickets had been sold.
19 It isn't fair to .... the unemployed.
20 He doesn't work in this office; I'll .... to his extension.
21 He just can't seem to .... his wife's death, the poor man.
22 So you don't like my idea! Can you .... something better?
23 We .... of petrol and had to walk five miles to the nearest garage.
24 I'm not telling you to stop smoking entirely; I just think you should ....
25 He was shot for .... his country's military secrets.

Functions

Often it is useful to look at language in terms of what we do with it, i.e.: its 'function', as well as its structure.

Here is a list of key functional areas which are dealt with in *Think Ahead to First Certificate*. Turn to the references and write down some examples. The references direct you to the pages where they are dealt with in the most depth, although there are many examples of the different functions throughout the course.

Agreeing and disagreeing UNIT 9, SET D.

....

Asking indirect questions UNIT 4, SET D.

....

Comparing and contrasting UNIT 7, SET C.

....

Describing ability UNIT 6, SET D.

....

Describing dress UNIT 1, SET A.

....

Describing geographical features/a country
UNIT 11, SET A.

....

Describing objects UNIT 4, SET D; UNIT 4, SET E.

....

Describing past and present habits
UNIT 2, SET C. *(used to do/ing)*

....

Describing people: faces UNIT 7, SET A.

....

Describing a process UNIT 11, SET D.

....

Describing a room UNIT 15, SET C.

....

Describing a painting UNIT 6, SET B.

....

Expressing number and quantity UNIT 4, SET A.

....

Expressing obligation UNIT 14, SET B.

....

Expressing plans and intentions UNIT 10, SET A.

....

Expressing opinions UNIT 6, SET B.

....

Expressing reason and purpose
UNIT 2, SET B. *(so/because)*

....

Expressing sympathy UNIT 13, SET B.

....

Giving instructions UNIT 1, SET E.

....

Giving and requesting advice
UNIT 5, SET B; UNIT 10, SET D.

....

Giving street directions UNIT 8, SET D.

....

Making complaints UNIT 1, SET C.

....

Making decisions UNIT 10, SET A.

....

Making polite requests UNIT 8, SET D.

....

Making predictions UNIT 10, SET A.

....

Making questions UNIT 2, SET B; UNIT 8, SET A.

....

Making suggestions/agreeing and disagreeing with suggestions UNIT 2, SET A.

....

Narrating UNIT 3, SET E.

....

Ordering actions
UNIT 1, SET E. *(after/afterwards/after that)*

....

Ordering actions
UNIT 2, SET B. *(then, finally, first of all)*

....

Telephoning UNIT 3, SET D.

....

'Language Study' Index

Turn to the references given and complete the examples to make your own 'Language Study' Index.

Adjective order: UNIT 4, SET E.

Adjective + preposition: UNIT 7, SET C.
Ratan Patel is .... languages.

After and *afterwards*: UNIT 1, SET E.
I put the blindfold on her. .... I went into the audience.
.... I had put the blindfold on her, I went into the audience.

Countable and uncountable: UNIT 4, SET A.
I'm looking for .... treasure.
.... luck have you had so far?
Well ....

Describing physical appearance: UNIT 7, SET A.
Angela .... beautiful blue eyes, long red hair, pale skin and freckles.
Mr Gilbert, a big man .... a bald head and glasses.

Despite and *although*: UNIT 4, SET C.
.... the poor man's warning, Shovell kept on his course.
.... he escaped drowning, he was murdered.

Different types of description: UNIT 9, SET B.
What's she like?
How is she?
What does she look like?
What does she like?

Expressing ability: UNIT 6, SET D.
She .... to hum the melody.

First and second conditional: UNIT 8, SET C.
.... you move to Rome, ... a Roman too.
.... you moved to Rome, ... a Roman too.

Future predictions: UNIT 13, SET C.
A few specially chosen human beings .... Earth.
Civilization ....

Going to or *will?*: UNIT 10, SET A.
.... a policeman when I grow up.

Have something done and *need*: UNIT 15, SET B.
She .... her picture .... by a professional photographer.
The roof .... repairing.

If, unless and *otherwise*: UNIT 5, SET A.
.... you don't eat more fruit, your teeth will fall out!
.... you eat more fruit, your teeth will fall out!
You..................... eat more fruit .... your teeth will fall out!

In case: UNIT 10, SET D.
I'll take a map .... I get lost.

Indefinite pronouns: UNIT 7, SET B.
Say you're sorry when you hurt ....
Share ....

Indirect questions: UNIT 4, SET D.
Could you tell me where he was from?
Do you know what it's worth?

Infinitive and the gerund: UNIT 3, SET B.
Casanova .... him quiet.
They .... one of the roof-tiles.

Linking, explaining and contrasting: UNIT 13, SET D.

Make and *let*: UNIT 14, SET B.
She and the Prime Minister tried to .... Edward end the relationship.
Public opinion would not .... a twice-divorced American woman become Queen.

Making intelligent guesses: UNIT 13, SET B.
You .... tired.
It .... a change in the weather.

Narrative tenses: UNIT 3, SET E.
Paul .... drinks at the bar, when disaster struck.
Within seconds, a fire .... and .... to lots of gas-filled balloons, which .... to explode.
Paul .... to me at midnight.

Passive: UNIT 11, SET C.
They .... the hostile tribes of the Lower Xingu.

Tapescripts

■ SET A ■ PAGE 7

Women's fashions since the 1950s

1 In this photograph she's wearing a pinkish patterned shirt and trousers. They're quite short and stop above her ankle. She's also wearing a pair of sandals. Her hair is up and she seems to be wearing a lot of make-up and, um, false eyelashes. Looks quite nice, I suppose.

2 Um, I think this is really fashionable. Really simple but very smart and practical too. She has just got on a black one piece suit and a pair of white trainers. She has got long straight hair and is wearing some bright red lipstick. Apart from that no other make-up.

3 She looks really weird in this one. I mean, lots of black lipstick and her hair is in a mess. She is wearing trousers and a loose yellow top with a scarf tied around her waist. She looks a bit like a pirate. Awful.

4 Wow! This one is really too much. She is wearing a really short skirt and high heeled shoes. She has also got on a leopard skin top. Hope it wasn't from a real leopard. You could have worn this to a party but not for anything else surely.

5 This must be the oldest one. She is formally dressed and looks terribly old fashioned. She is wearing a matching skirt and jacket with high-heeled shoes and she is carrying a tiny bag and has got a funny little hat on her head. Her clothes look really tight and uncomfortable.

■ SET E ■ PAGE 14

A 'Mentalist Act'

Int: How did you start in show business, Arthur?

AC: As a magician's assistant for 'The Great Marvella'. I helped out mostly with the mentalist act.

Int: What was that?

AC: Oh, a kind of telepathic act where she guessed the names of objects while wearing a blindfold. Um... I put the blindfold on her. Afterwards I went into the audience. People handed me objects like watches or rings and things and then 'The Great Marvella' guessed what they were.

Int: And how did this trick work then? She didn't have any special powers, did she?

AC: No, not at all. Actually she could see through the cloth.

Int: So it was as simple as that!

AC: Not really. After I had blindfolded her she couldn't actually see the objects. They were too small, and don't forget the theatres were dark.

Int: So how was it done?

AC: I spelled out the name of the object by the way that I was standing. For example, if I had my head on the left, that told her that it began with 'r'; or if both of my arms were bent that there was an 'ing' sound in the word...

Int: So she could guess that you'd been given a ring. And did anybody ever realize what you were doing?

AC: No. Never. I also misled the audience. I said things in a funny way – you know – changed my intonation so that people would think I was signalling with my voice.

Int: Clever. And did it work? I mean did the boss always manage to guess the objects which were handed to you?

AC: Oh yes. Ninety-five per-cent of the time.

Int: And for the other five?

AC: She just said that the vibrations weren't right. The audience loved it.

■ SET C ■ PAGE 20

The changing Mickey Mouse

Rachel: Oh great. *The Flintstones* are on telly. I used to watch *The Flintstones* when I was a kid.

Barry: Me too. My favourite's *Tom and Jerry* though.

Rachel: That's because of all the violence!

Barry: Don't be silly... It's just a cartoon!

Julia: But they are really cruel. I agree with Rachel.

Barry: It's just harmless fun!

Rachel: But kids still copy them. I mean, these things have, um, more of an effect than we like to think. *Tom and Jerry* seems to get more and more violent too.

Barry: Oh come off it! They're exactly the same...

Julia: That's not true you know. Characters do change. Take Mickey Mouse.

Barry: Mickey Mouse?

Rachel: Yeah, I read an article. It – the article – said in the old days, in the early cartoons he was really horrible. You know, he was always doing cruel things.

Barry: Cruel things?

Rachel: Yeah. Like, in one erm, cartoon he makes the animals play a tune by pinching and squeezing them, to erm make them squeal.

Julia: That's right. We're not used to seeing that kind of Mickey these days. He is too busy being nice to everybody.

Barry: Goody goody.

Julia: Right – He never does anything naughty.

Barry: Even so. This article, did it say anything else?

Rachel: I'm trying to think. Oh yeah – it said that his face gets rounder and softer as time goes on.... How can I explain? Have you seen any of the early cartoons?

Julia and Barry: Yes.

Rachel: Well, in the early ones he looks quite rat-like, doesn't he? He has got this long pointed nose and little eyes.

Barry: And?

Rachel: Well later on his face changes. His head gets as big as his body. Or almost. His eyes get bigger, too.

Barry: Strange, isn't it?

Rachel: Yeah, he grows backwards! He gets younger instead of older. I wonder if they did it on purpose?

Julia: Mm, it makes him much cuter I suppose.

Barry: An acceptable symbol for the US of A.

UNIT 3

■ SET C   ■ PAGE 29

A narrow escape

Janice: Goodness! That was lucky... It reminds me of one I had years ago. I was studying Italian in Rome.

Carole: Huh, huh.

Janice: One erm night I went to a to a pop, pop concert in an indoor stadium. We all set off in a party mood; we'd been looking forward to it for ages. Anyway, around this time people used to invade cinemas and theatres without paying because they said prices were just too high.

Carole: Sounds like a good idea.

Janice: Not if you'd paid. Well that evening, about two hundred of them got in. Every seat was taken. It was packed.

Carole: Go on.

Janice: So then the riot police turned up and told everybody to leave. Then the troublemakers started throwing things at the police. They'd come prepared for a fight, they had sticks and helmets. Fighting broke out around the stadium.

Carole: Wow!

Janice: Then the police starting hitting their sticks against their shields. It was a really terrifying noise. Anyway, the troublemakers kept throwing things at them and several got hurt by flying chairs and things. Eventually they just ran out of patience and started firing tear gas and hitting people.

Carole: What just the troublemakers?

Janice: No anybody... Discipline just broke down.

Carole: ... and did you get hurt?

Janice: Almost. A policeman told me to move but I answered back in English. Roberto did though. He got hit on the head so I stayed by him until he came round. Finally we got away, they hadn't blocked off one of the exits. Of course we were coughing and blind from the tear gas but it was great to get outside.

■ SET D   ■ PAGE 31

Booking by telephone

Part A

Telephonist: Breakaway Travel.

Mrs Roberts: Good morning, I'm phoning about your weekend escapes to Berlin.

Telephonist: I'll put you through to someone who can help you. Hold the line please, madam. I'm afraid all lines are busy. If you'd like to leave me your name and number I'll get someone to return your call as soon as possible.

Mrs Roberts: The name is Mrs Roberts and my number is 675982.

Telephonist: Right Mrs Roberts I'll pass the message on.

Part B

Five minutes later

Mrs Roberts: Hello. 675982.

Sharon Grey: Hello. This is Sharon from Breakaway Travel...

Mrs Roberts: Oh hello, thanks for ringing back. I'd like to know about your weekend escapes to Berlin for the last weekend of next month.

Sharon Grey: Let me see. Yes, madam, three nights departing the 27th is available. That's £320 per person for scheduled flights and a double room in a three star hotel with continental breakfast is also included.

Mrs Roberts: That sounds fine. I'll come in to book this afternoon.

Sharon Grey: I look forward to seeing you then, Mrs Roberts.

Mrs Roberts: Goodbye.

UNIT 4

■ SET B   ■ PAGE 37

Sunken treasure

PJ: So Frances, is there very much pirate treasure left?

FG: I'm not sure. You see they mostly spent what they stole or else it was taken back. Kidd's famous treasure might not even exist. But there are lots of sunken wrecks out there.

PJ: Sunken treasure. That's really romantic. What advice would you give listeners who want to get rich quick?

FG: Basically I'd tell them not to bother. The ships carrying it often sank in bad weather. Then over the next few hundred years they move and get covered in sand.

PJ: All the same, it's just lying out there waiting for someone to pick it up!

FG: Well, treasure hunting is a bit more complicated than that. For one thing it's an incredibly expensive activity. It nearly always ends in disappointment too.

PJ: I see, but there are success stories, aren't there? I seem to remember one where lots of porcelain was found.

FG: Mm, that was the Dutch ship the 'Geldermalsen'.

PJ: The thing that amazed me was that it was in such fantastic condition.

FG: Yes, it looks new, doesn't it? That's because it had been packed in tea which was the rest of the cargo.

PJ: Oh, right. Have there been any other big finds?

FG: Quite a few. Mostly because of improvements in technology. One of the biggest was in 1985 off the coast of Florida. Someone called Mel Fisher found the wreck of a galleon called 'La Nuestra Senora de Atocha'.

PJ: Did he find it while he was fishing or something?

FG: Not quite. Actually he had been looking for it for fifteen years! It has been worth it because so far they have recovered over four hundred and fifty million dollars worth of silver.

PJ: But it's not the biggest?

FG: Actually no. That's the Russian treasure ship the 'Admiral Nakhimov'. It was sunk during the Russian-Japanese war at the beginning of the century. Its cargo was two billion dollars worth of gold and platinum.

PJ: Wow!

■ SET D   ■ PAGE 40

Treasure in our attic

1

George Brown: Well, hello young man, and what's your name?

Robin: Robin.

George Brown: And how old are you then?

Robin's mother: He was seven last week.

George Brown: Seven eh! What have you brought to show us? It's a lovely old teddy bear. It's golden brown but the poor chap's fur's rather worn now and one of his eyes is loose. Where did you get it from Robin?

Robin: My grandfather gave it to me. It was his when he was little.

George Brown: Could you tell me where he was from?

Robin's mother: Actually, he was German.

George Brown: Just as I thought. And if we look at the bear's ear we should find a little button with the manufacturer's name. Yes here we are. Do you know what you have here?

Robin's mother: Grandad Martin's teddy, I suppose.

George Brown: But it's very special. You see this is a very early teddy made by Margaret Steiff in Germany. She is the lady who invented the teddy bear. Now what do you think it's worth?

Robin's mother: A few pounds? I've no idea really.

George Brown: Well, let me tell you something. Young Robin is a lucky young man. These bears are quite valuable. This one is worth about a thousand pounds.

Robin's mother: Do you know if someone would like to buy it?

Robin: Come on mummy, give me back my teddy bear. He's mine...

2

Rupert Andrews: Yes, sir. What is it we have here? Let's have a look. Um. I have just been handed an old golf ball. It's not often you see one of these. Can I ask where you got it?

Mr Crown: I actually came across it in the attic along with some old clubs and other things, but I just thought I'd bring this in to show you.

Rupert Andrews: Well, I'm extremely glad that you did. If I can just describe it to the listeners at home. It's not perfectly smooth like one of the plastic coated golf balls we have these days. In fact it is made of pieces of leather which have been stitched together. This is a real collector's item. A year or two ago a ball similar to this was sold for four thousand pounds! This one is rather cracked I'm afraid but is still valuable. It just goes to show that you should never throw anything away; most people would take one look at this and think it was worthless. Personally, I find an antiques handbook an invaluable source of useful information.

3

George Brown: Now what do we have here? It is a figure of Charlie Chaplin... um... It looks like one which was made in England in around 1918. Oh dear. Unfortunately it isn't genuine. I'm afraid that it is an imitation. A real one would be worth around two thousand pounds now. Never mind. This doesn't make this entirely worthless. I would say you could probably get around fifty pounds for it. Would you mind telling me how much you paid for it?

Man: Not really, I suppose, it cost me ninety pounds.

George Brown: Pity.

4

Rupert Andrews: A young lady has just brought me something which a lot of people will be interested in. It's an early Beatles record which was issued in the mid-sixties. Where did you get this young lady?

Girl: It belongs to my dad.

Rupert Andrews: Well. What makes this interesting is that it has all of the Beatles' signatures on it and is signed 'All the Best George Harrison'. Are they genuine?

Girl: Yeah. My dad got it from George Harrison. He was working as a waiter in a hotel and he asked them if they'd sign it for him.

Rupert Andrews: Do you know what it's worth?

Girl: Well, as far as my dad's concerned it's priceless, he'd never part with it.

Rupert Andrews: Well he might if you tell him it could be worth around a thousand pounds at auction.

Girl: A thousand pounds. Wow!

UNIT 5

SET C   PAGE 48

An interview with an iridologist

Annie: So how long have you been an iridologist?

Paola: Oh, I've been practising for about seven years now.

Annie: And do you have an ordinary medical background too?

Paola: Actually yes, I have been a pharmacist, I trained as one and practised for a few years.

Annie: Really? Why did you give up?

Paola: I decided to stop when I noticed how many people are made made sick by the medicines they are prescribed.

Annie: What, from the side effects?

Paola: Not just that. Fortunately, I have never taken sleeping pills in in my life but lots of people get addicted to them.

Annie: How come this happens?

Paola: Quite simply the doctor often makes the wrong diagnosis. The wrong medicine is prescribed to people who are already ill and weak.

Annie: So that explains why you're fed up with conventional medicine; but why iridology?

Paola: Because it gives an accurate diagnosis and cares about prevention as much as cure. Conventional medicine is only interested in you once you get sick.

Annie: Mm, I'm not sure that's always true. But anyway, how can you tell someone's health by looking at their eyes?

Paola: We start with the colour which tells us about your basic constitution. Erm... people with blue eyes tend to have allergies and rheumatism, things like that. Those with brown eyes have problems with circulation and their digestion.

Annie: Huh, huh. And what about hazel eyes like yours?

Paola: Well, hazel and green eyes are actually false colours. Hazel is a mixture of brown on blue. Green eyes are also basically blue but liver problems gives them a yellow overlay.

Annie: And what can you tell from my eyes?

Paola: OK then... Mm... Now, eyes wide open, look straight in front good. Well, you've got a good constitution. There's something wrong with your left knee though. I can see that you have hurt it at some time.

Annie: Goodness! That's right. I had quite a bad skiing accident two years ago, I had an operation but it has bothered me ever since. How on earth did you see that?

Paola: Well there's a mark on the iris here at about six o'clock... let me show you on the chart.

Annie: Well, that's quite incredible, I'll have to come to you for a consultation. And can you see....

UNIT 6

SET B   PAGE 54

In an art gallery

Phil: What do you think of this, Jane?

Jane: Ugh! I think it's awful, I don't like it at all.

Phil: Why on earth not? I think it's fascinating.

Jane: It's just a lot of funny black lines. It does nothing for me. Ah, but look! What a marvellous picture! All those gorgeous colours.

Phil: Do you really think so? You have never seen grass that colour. It's terrible.

Jane: But it's not supposed to be realistic. Anyway, let's not argue. Do you like this one over here?

Phil: Oh yes, fantastic. That's what I call a painting.

SET D ■ PAGE 58
The sad geniuses

Unfortunately some children will never be able to lead ordinary lives because they have serious mental and physical disabilities. However, a tiny few are able to do things that ordinary people would find quite impossible. Take the case of Ellen Boudreaux. When she was four months old doctors realized she was completely blind. Yet two months later her parents noticed something extraordinary. Above her bed she had one of those musical toys which plays a tune. Ellen could copy it exactly by humming the tune. Other incredible things followed. Little Ellen couldn't walk until she was four. However, when she finally started she managed to get around without knocking into anything even though she was blind. Even outside in woods and forests she just knows where all the trees are and can avoid them. When she walks about she makes a little noise. Some doctors believe it is her own personal kind of radar. But let's go back to her remarkable musical ability. Ellen learned how to play the piano and the guitar like an expert. But what is amazing is her musical memory. She only has to hear a piece of music once and she can reproduce it exactly. What's more, she never forgets anything and can play and sing all the songs she has ever heard. These abilities are extraordinary particularly if we remember that she can't hold a simple conversation, she can only echo and repeat questions. All doctors also agree that she has a very low intelligence. Yet she has one more miraculous gift I would like to tell you about. Ellen has an incredible 'internal clock' inside her brain which tells her to the second what the time is. This means she knows exactly when to turn the radio on for one of her favourite programmes.

UNIT 7

SET A ■ PAGE 61
Crime and punishment in the classroom

I don't think I'll ever forget what happened that day in 1975. I was just seven years old and had fallen deeply in love for the first time. Angela had beautiful blue eyes, long red hair, pale skin and freckles. While the teacher's back was turned, I passed her a note which said 'Angela, I love you – Tim.' She looked at it and at once put up her hand. 'Mr Gilbert,' she shouted, 'Tim has been naughty, he wrote this.' Mr Gilbert, a big man with a bald head and glasses took the note and looked at it. He smiled and I thought he was going to let the incident pass. Instead, he called me to the front of the class and told me to read the note aloud. As I said the words I felt so ashamed that my face turned a deep shade of red. All the other children laughed and I returned to my desk. However, this was not the end of it, each time he turned away from the class to write something on the board Angela turned towards me and stuck out her tongue. After the seventh or eighth time I stood up, picked up a heavy dictionary and did something which would have the most terrible consequences....

SET D ■ PAGE 66
A miraculous way to learn?

Part A

Kay Able: What is this fast method for learning languages, doctor?

Dr Green: Basically it gets us to use all our brain. The brain is divided into two halves. Each half has different jobs. The left half is the logical side. This is where language is stored. The right side deals with space, artistic ability and music.

Part B

Kay Able: So artists and musicians use the powers in the right half.

Dr Green: ... that's correct. Now, most teaching methods depend on studying grammar and doing exercises. There is also a lot of repetition. This is all logical left brain activity.

Kay Able: But what's wrong with that?

Dr Green: Well, what happens is that students work hard but often don't learn a lot. By the next lesson they can hardly remember anything. It's slow. What they need to do is use all of their brain.

Kay Able: How exactly can you do this?

Dr Green: Well, you know how we can remember rhymes and songs from childhood...

Kay Able: Mm yes. The other day I sang a song to a child which I last heard, it must have been twenty years ago. I was surprised I could still remember it.

Dr Green: Well, it doesn't surprise me. The two halves of your brain were working together. The words were kept in the left part but you were able to remember them because the music from the right side helped to fix them there.

Part C

Kay Able: So we should learn languages through singing?

Dr Green: Not exactly, but let me quickly say something about the method which was invented by a Bulgarian professor called Lozanov. His method has lately been developed in the United States. The teacher speaks to the students using a special rhythm and intonation which helps us to remember the language longer. The lesson is also accompanied by slow music. All these things make the brain work more efficiently and the language learning process faster, easier and much less stressful.

Kay Able: So the two halves work together. It sounds fantastic. I think I'll take up German again.

Dr Green: It's never too late to learn, Kay.

UNIT 8

SET A ■ PAGE 68
City thoughts

1 Oh no! This looks like trouble... He's coming towards us. What's *that* in his hand... we should have taken a cab.

2 Either you don't exist or they beat you like an animal in a zoo. Tourists! What do you expect – a big smile? You've got your photo – now how about some change?

3 What a jam! I'll never get my flight. The only thing that's moving is the meter in this funny old taxi.

4 Whee, this is great. What a neat birthday gift!

5 Drivers. Think they own the road; and all the pollution. I'm glad I've got this mask... The lights are going to change! Just watch me beat this guy!

SET B   PAGE 71
Two cities

Part A

Poppy: This is a lovely house, Mrs Hallam. Is it very old?

Mrs Hallam: Quite old. It's Victorian, you know, it was built about a hundred years ago. There are thousands like it. You see, in the last century London grew enormously.

Poppy: But how did people get to work?

Mrs Hallam: By train. People have moved further and further out. Loads of people commute. The quality of life is often much better. They can live in the countryside and maybe have a bigger house. You escape all of the social problems we have here.

Poppy: Social problems. What do you mean?

Mrs Hallam: Well, during my childhood it was lovely round here. Nowadays there's quite a bit of crime.

Poppy: Crime! Goodness! What kind of thing?

Mrs Hallam: Burglaries, and muggings too. You see, you've got people like me who are reasonably well-off, then unemployed and homeless people. You have to be careful at night.

Poppy: Oh dear. And what else?

Mrs Hallam: There's all the litter and the dirty streets.

Poppy: You make it sound terrible! Why on earth do you stay?

Mrs Hallam: Because I love it really. You've got the theatre here, all of the cinemas and museums and things. It's interesting too, just wandering around the streets. There are lots of lovely parks as well. We moved out into the country for a while but we were bored. It was green and beautiful and everything but it was just too quiet I suppose.

Part B

Mrs Hallam: Anyway, tell me about Athens. I went when I was a girl. I had a marvellous time sightseeing. It was marvellous – I'll always remember it.

Poppy: Well, I think it must have changed since you were there. We've got our problems too. Pollution mainly. There are too many cars. Sometimes Athens is just one big traffic jam. Sometimes we're covered by a yellow cloud we call the 'nefos'.

Mrs Hallam: ...sounds like London in the fifties with our smog.

Poppy: It's terrible for the buildings like the Parthenon. The stone is just being eaten away.

Mrs Hallam: Oh dear. Can't the government do something?

Poppy: Well, it tried to cut down traffic in the centre. You can only go in every other day; according to whether your number plate is odd or even.

Mrs Hallam: Has it worked?

Poppy: It has helped a bit.

Mrs Hallam: What would you do if you were in charge?

Poppy: First of all I'd try to improve public transport, then...

UNIT 9

SET B   PAGE 79
Describing someone

Carmen: It's really kind of you to offer to meet my aunt.

....

Carmen: Well, she's quite short and plump. She's about fifty-five and has got curly grey hair. She wears glasses and loves bright clothes.

....

Carmen: Really nice. Very lively. I haven't seen her since my Uncle Pablo died.

....

Carmen: Oh yes. She was very sad at first but she's OK now.

....

Carmen: She doesn't speak a word. You'll be able to practise your Spanish.

....

Carmen: She adores shopping. The last time she came to England we went to Harrods. I'm sure she'd love to go again..

SET D   PAGE 83
Agreeing and disagreeing

Simon: Mm ... he is just one kind of Englishman. Lots of black people are English too. Another thing, nobody dresses like him these days.

Shirley: That's just not true. What about on the tube every morning. All those businessmen and civil servants?

Simon: Alright... but the other day I went to the post office and there was this guy – you know behind the counter – a civil servant – and he had punkish hair and an earring.

Shirley: Did it bother you, the hair and that?

Simon: Not really. Surprised that's all...

Shirley: Mm. You might be right. Anyway, that bit about the typical English family, you know, dad at work, mum at home, I thought that was wrong.

Simon: Why's that?

Shirley: Well, a lot of kids are only brought up by one parent. Dad's living with someone else....

Simon: ... he's not in the garden with his roses.

Shirley: Right, that bit about the daughter living with a punk was realistic ... It always seems to happen with middle class families, doesn't it?

Simon: Yeah, you're right. For me the best thing about the article was that it made me wonder what foreigners think of us. I'm sure if you spoke to them about the English gentleman they'd laugh.

Shirley: Absolutely, all those awful English holidaymakers. Mm, they probably think the typical Englishman is a drunk football fan....

Simon: That's right, wearing union jack swimming trunks and reading a copy of *The Sun*.

UNIT 10

SET A   PAGE 86
Toad-in-the-hole!

Moira: I wonder where Poppy is. I hope she hasn't got lost.

Martin: I'm sure she'll be here soon. Let's look at the menu.

Moira: I think I'll have the smoked salmon then the duck. What about you, darling?

Martin: I'll have the cheese and onion tart and the roast beef.

Poppy: Hello. Sorry I'm late. I got lost.

Martin: Never mind. Do sit down.

....

Moira: Well, Yorkshire pudding – it's a sort of cake made from eggs and flour and water. You cook it in the oven and eat it when it's crisp and brown...

Poppy: Oh, I think I see. And toad-in-the-hole? What a strange name!

Moira: Oh that's Yorkshire pudding with sausages cooked inside.

Poppy: I see. I really can't make up my mind.
Moira: Why don't you have the duck? That's what I am going to have.
Poppy: Alright then. And I'd like to start with the soup.
Waiter: Are you ready to order, sir?
Martin: Yes, I think so. Will you bring us a bottle of dry white wine with the first course and we're going to have...

Poppy: Thank you for a lovely meal. It was really delicious. I am afraid I am going to have to go.
Martin: What so soon?
Poppy: I am sorry to leave in such a hurry but I am worried about getting home.
Martin: Come on, stay for coffee. It's going to rain soon and you'll get soaked. We'll give you a lift.

◼ SET B ◼ PAGE 88
How to make bread-and-butter pudding

Now today's quick recipe is for bread and butter pudding. It's a simple but delicious dessert. Now, you'll need the following ingredients: three quarters of a litre of milk, two hundred grams of butter, four large or six small eggs, two hundred and fifty grams of sugar, some dried sultanas, the big juicy ones, you'll need about one hundred and fifty grams – or if you can't get sultanas some little raisins. Oh, and I almost forgot you'll need about half a dozen slices of white bread, it's actually better if it's a day old.

So what you do is this, break the eggs into a bowl and mix in the sugar, then add the milk and beat the mixture well until it's nice and smooth. Now take the slices of bread and spread them generously with butter, cut off the crust and cut each slice into three or four strips. Take a medium sized shallow dish, something that can go in the oven and butter it so that it doesn't stick. Then put the strips of buttered bread along the bottom of the dish to form a layer. Take about half the sultanas or raisins and sprinkle them on... you can be quite generous. Then put down another layer of bread and butter strips and sprinkle on the rest of the sultanas. Now pour the egg and milk mixture over the bread and butter and sultanas and leave it for a couple of hours. Then, when the bread is nice and wet, put it in a medium hot oven, around two hundred degrees for about forty-five minutes or until it starts to rise and go nice and crisp. It's best not to eat it straight away, I think it tastes much better if it's warm rather than boiling hot.

◼ SET C ◼ PAGE 90
Watch your body language

Carol Jones: When we're abroad, it's not just the spoken language that can cause problems. Most travellers can remember accidentally upsetting someone because a gesture which is harmless at home, causes great offence abroad. On 'Travel Wise' today we have Dr Ian Williams, an expert on international gestures.
Dr Williams: Good evening.
Carol Jones: Now, Ian. I believe that even experts like you are sometimes caught out.
Dr Williams: Oh indeed, Carol. Why, I remember being in India and misunderstanding a conversation. You see the person I was talking to kept shaking his head. I thought he was disagreeing with me. In fact it turned out to be the opposite.
Carol Jones: So his head shake meant yes?
Dr Williams: More than that, it meant 'carry on talking because I'm interested'.

Carol Jones: So we can't even take simple head movements for granted. What about closer to home?
Dr Williams: Well, in Europe some gestures are universal. Thumbing your nose means the same whether you are in Oslo or Madrid. But very often a gesture is either unknown or else means something entirely different. For example the thumbs up sign we use to mean OK is known throughout northern Europe. But if you go to Greece or Italy people won't understand what you're on about.
Carol Jones: Mm... talking of Italy I'm reminded of that strange gesture, you know, the one where they hold the tips of their fingers together and move them up and down...
Dr Williams: Oh yes, the 'hand purse'. Um, we never see it over here but it's used all around the Mediterranean. Unfortunately it's probably the most confusing gesture around.
Carol Jones: Why's that?
Dr Williams: Well in Italy you'll remember it means 'What are you getting at?' or 'I don't understand'... Yet in France it can mean that you are afraid, and if you go to Greece it means that something is good, while in Spain it simply means 'a lot'.
Carol Jones: What a minefield! Sadly, the news is about to begin, so we don't have time to go into this any further. But Ian, what one piece of advice would you give to travellers going abroad?
Dr Williams: Never copy local gestures as it can seem strange and cause offence. Steer clear of local taboo gestures too.
Carol Jones: So probably the best thing on your next trip is to remember to keep your hands in your pockets. It's by far the safest way! Dr Ian Williams thank you for coming in. And now we go over to the newsroom where...

UNIT 11

◼ SET B ◼ PAGE 97
The world's favourite Australians

When explorers came to Australia they couldn't believe their eyes. **The** continent was full of strange and wonderful creatures. There was **the** kangaroo which moved along in huge jumps, and all kinds of new snakes and insects. **The** strangest one of all was **the** duck-billed platypus, basically because nobody could work out what it was. Let me explain why.

It's a bit like **a** duck because it has got **a** bill and webbed feet and lays eggs. It spends most of its time in **the** water digging around in **the** mud with its bill but instead of feathers it is covered with fur so it can't be **a** bird. In the end scientists decided it was **a** mammal because it is warm-blooded and produces milk for its young.

Everybody's favourite, though, is the koala bear. Koalas are rather interesting. They are active at night and because of this, spend most of the daytime asleep in the fork of trees. They don't have tails which is strange for animals which live in trees but they have a hard pad of skin which lets them sit for hours. They have pouches for their young like kangaroos but theirs open downwards! Baby koalas spend about six months in the pouches before riding on their mothers' backs.

Over the past two hundred years they have had a varied history... In the old days dingoes ate them and they were hunted by the aborigines. When the Europeans colonized Australia they shot the dingoes and the aborigines started eating different food. This was great for the koalas and the population grew incredibly. Unfortunately they were hunted for their fur and in 1924 two million koala skins were exported.

Nowadays, they are no longer hunted but there are other dangers. Koalas eat enormous amounts of leaves from gum trees but since many of the forests have been cut down food is getting scarce. Disease and cars are two other major threats. Luckily people are aware of the problems and are trying to protect them so their future doesn't look too bad.

Even though they look so cute and cuddly don't be taken in! One famous politician saw a koala and picked it up for a group of photographers. The koala wasn't interested and scratched him with its sharp claws. By the way, in case you were wondering, the name 'koala' comes from the aborigine language which means: 'I don't drink'. Even though they can drink water, they get most of the liquid they need from the leaves they eat.

■ SET D   ■ PAGE 100
Don't be so green!

Frank: Just look at these pictures! Why doesn't your government do something?
Maria: Are you accusing me of burning down the forest again?
Frank: It's somebody's fault. You can't blame us.
Maria: But I do. Indirectly you're responsible. Your banks lent us too much. And we can't pay it back…
Frank: What are you getting at?
Maria: Well, interest rates are high and we're desperate for dollars. We have to clear the forest to provide land for cattle.
Frank: That's still no excuse. You shouldn't have borrowed so much. Anyway. What about coffee? Couldn't you export that?
Maria: We do. But there's more money in beef than coffee.
Frank: Come off it! I paid two pounds sixty p for this jar.
Maria: But we get hardly anything… about fifty p, I think.
Frank: How come?
Maria: It's the processing – the roasting and the grinding – which adds value. That's done over here.
Frank: So why not process it yourselves? Or put up the price?
Maria: Because importing countries are too powerful.
Frank: Even so… there must be another way.
Maria: Yes and no. You can't prevent people from clearing the forest if that's the only way they've got of making a living. We have to show there's an alternative by encouraging people to buy more products which grow in the forest; you know – like nuts and rubber.
Frank: No morality, just economics. You're a hard woman, Maria.
Maria: And you, Frank, darling… sometimes you're just a bit too green!

UNIT 12

■ SET A   ■ PAGE 103
How to get an interview

Julian: What's so funny?
Annabel: It's this book. It's about this journalist who would do anything for a story.
Julian: Who did he work for?
Annabel: The tabloids, the popular papers.
Julian: One of those..
Annabel: Anyway, he got up to some real tricks.
Julian: Like what?
Annabel: Well, you know Oliver Reed?
Julian: The film director?

Annabel: That's Oliver Stone. Oliver Reed, the actor.
Julian: Oh him? … a bit of a playboy wasn't he?
Annabel: Mm that's right. There was a lot of gossip a few years ago, he married a schoolgirl…
Julian: Who, Wensley what's his name?
Annabel: No, Oliver Reed.
Julian: What! He must have been twice her age.
Annabel: Three times, actually. Anyway, Wensley, you know, the journalist, he realized that this would be a great story so he followed them to the West Indies.
Julian: Oliver Reed can't have been happy.
Annabel: You're right. He refused to talk to anyone. Of course Wensley couldn't go back to England without a story – his editor would have killed him.
Julian: I can imagine…
Annabel: Anyway Wensley was desperate. What he did was invite Reed's minder, you know a kind of bodyguard, to his hotel.
Julian: Crafty.
Annabel: And guess what. His minder actually turned up with the girl and Wensley got them to tell him the whole story!
Julian: And where was Reed while this was going on?
Annabel: At home in bed with a cold. Anyway, the best bit is that Wensley told the other two…
Julian: The girl and the minder?
Annabel: Yeah… so he told them that he was going out to get some food because everyone was feeling hungry. Anyway, instead, he went off to find Reed. He just walked into the villa.
Julian: What a cheek!
Annabel: Reed was furious and chased him out of the house. All the while though, Wensley was asking him questions.
Julian: And did he get him?
Annabel: No, he got away, although Reed spent the next day checking every hotel on the island. It was worth it though, Wensley had his interview and his editor was happy. The story made the headlines.

■ SET D   ■ PAGE 108
The news

This is the eight o'clock news on Wednesday 1st April. First the main news headlines read by Arthur Robinson.

★ New regulations for Britain's motorists are to come into force from midnight tonight.
★ A blaze has destroyed examination buildings in Cambridge.
★ Bad weather has caused the destruction of Italy's spaghetti crop.

And now for the news in depth from your newscaster Annie McCleod.

The minister of transport Mr Alfred Murphy has announced that as of midnight tonight new regulations for road users will come into force. From midnight cars and buses will have to drive on the right-hand side of the road. To avoid unnecessary confusion bicycles and lorries will not have to comply with the changeover until February 29th of next year. All traffic will be banned from roads between 11.30 this evening and midnight to ensure that the changeover goes smoothly.

A blaze at the Local Examinations Board has destroyed a wing of the building. The mystery fire broke out at around three o'clock this morning and it took until nine o'clock for firefighters to bring it under control. Fortunately damage appears to be limited to the science examinations section. A spokesperson has said that a thousand, I'm sorry I'll read that again, a hundred thousand candidates who took the November examinations will have to re-sit. A group of students is helping police with their enquiries.

Bad weather has caused the destruction of this year's spaghetti crop in Northern Italy. The crop was destroyed by exceptionally cold weather for this time of year. Farmers woke up this morning to find that the spaghetti had frozen on the branches of their trees. This means ruin for thousands of Italian farmers who were depending on this year's harvest to rescue them from economic difficulties. This is the third year that the spaghetti harvest has been a disaster and farmers must be wondering if they will be rescued by the European Community again.

UNIT 13

SET B   PAGE 112
Living dinosaurs!

Part B

Pop Osborne: So did you have a nice time, Katie?
Katie: Yeah. It was great. Can I tell you all about dinosaurs?
Pop Osborne: If you like, dear.
Katie: Well, they died a long time ago. Sixty million years.
Pop Osborne: Well fancy that.
Katie: I bet you don't know why they died.
Pop Osborne: You are going to tell me anyway, I expect.
Katie: Well, people used to think it might have been a change in the weather. You know an ice-age.
Pop Osborne: Oh really.
Katie: Nowadays they think it could have been a meteor.
Pop Osborne: A meteor, from outer space? Why's that?
Katie: 'Cos lots of other things died at the same time. They know that 'cos geologists dug up lots of fossils of things that died. So it must have happened suddenly.
Pop Osborne: Fancy that. People have some funny ideas, don't they?
Katie: So what happened is that it fell in the sea – splash – and made it boil.
Pop Osborne: Well I never.
Katie: There was lots of steam and stuff. It killed most of the plants. The 'vegetarian' dinosaurs died out so did the meat eaters – like tyrannosaurus rex – he was a meat eater – he's my favourite – well they all died. It got too humid too.
Pop Osborne: I don't like the heat either!
Katie: But you're not a reptile! Dinosaurs were reptiles; you know, cold-blooded like snakes. We're mammals.
Pop Osborne: That's nice.
Katie: So the dinosaurs couldn't cope. The heat made them slow.
Pop Osborne: Oh dear!
Katie: But the mammals, they were warm-blooded, they could control their temperature better. My dad says they were our ancestors. But the dinosaurs they died!
Pop Osborne: What a shame. Who would have imagined it? The poor old dinosaurs.
Katie: Well, mum says we shouldn't feel sorry for them. They did last over a hundred and sixty million years!
Pop Osborne: Even so it can't have been nice for them. Anyway, talking of vegetarians and meat eaters what do you want for lunch? Spaghetti or a hamburger?

SET D   PAGE 117
The evolution of armour

Unfortunately human beings have always been very good at finding new ways of killing each other. When weapons improve and become more effective armour has to improve too.

(slide one)
In classical times most fighting was done on foot by soldiers fighting hand to hand with spears and swords. So armour had to give protection but be fairly light so the soldier could move. That's why armour from this period only protects the head and upper body.

(slide two)
This shows a beautiful helmet from Greece. Even though it covers most of the face there is still plenty of room for the soldier to see through.

(slide three)
In Roman times better equipped soldiers wore body armour made up of strips of metal which was far more flexible – each piece moves – they could move their bodies much more easily than in the armour made just from one piece.

(slide four)
During the Middle Ages, cavalry became more important and a lot of the fighting was done on horseback. This meant that armour could be heavier and give greater protection. A knight would wear a suit of chain mail which covered the whole body. Chain mail was popular for about four hundred years up to thirteen hundred. A knight would also have worn a heavy helmet like this one. It gave protection against heavy swords. Of course it was quite difficult to see because there was only a little hole to look through. However, as bows became more powerful they were able to penetrate chain mail so they had to find an alternative. The result was a return to plate armour.

(slide five)
For the next two hundred years, plate armour became more and more sophisticated. The best armour of all was made in Italy and Germany and shows remarkable craftsmanship.

(slide six)
The invention of gunpowder and guns changed the face of warfare. For a time it was possible to provide more protection by making thicker armour. But as guns improved armour became less and less effective.
Look at this breastplate from the English Civil War of the sixteen forties. The bullet has gone straight through and must have killed the poor soldier wearing it.

(slide seven)
People quickly realized that the best protection against a bullet is to be a fast moving and difficult target. Because of this, over the next few centuries we see a return to fast and lightly armed soldiers with very little protection.

(slide eight)
However, the last fifteen years or so have seen new developments. Some new materials are so strong that they can offer protection against bullets and flying metal. Look at this picture of an American foot soldier wearing a flak jacket and a helmet.

UNIT 14

■ SET D ■ PAGE 124

Henry VIII and his six wives

Int: Henry VIII was the founder of the royal navy and established the Church of England. However, he is best remembered for his six wives. He was a difficult man but was he as cruel as some people think?

B: Certainly. He was capable of tremendous cruelty. His reign is full of dead bodies. Wife number two – Anne Boleyn – and Catherine Howard wife number five both had their heads chopped off. Most of Catherine's family was executed too. Many ministers met the same fate. It seems to be the way he solved problems. However, we should remember this was a cruel age and it was common for princes to use their powers in this way.

Int: I see. And what made him marry so often?

B: Basically he was desperate for a son. His first wife Catherine of Aragon could only give him a daughter and so he had to re-marry. The Pope wouldn't let Henry divorce Catherine so Henry formed his own church so that he could go ahead with it anyway. It also gave him the excuse to close down all the monasteries and steal all their enormous wealth. His chief minister, Thomas Cromwell helped him with this.

Int: And what sort of reward did he get?

B: Well, for a long while Cromwell was the second most powerful man in the kingdom. Even though the great lords looked down on him as the son of a butcher they feared him. He made them obey the king and attend his special courts. But, as usual, in the end Henry turned on him and he lost his head.

Int: How come?

B: Well, Henry finally got a son from wife number three Jane Seymour. Sadly she died shortly after the birth so he was on the lookout for a wife again. English families either couldn't keep up with his demands or were suspicious of Henry. Diplomats had to look abroad. She couldn't be a Catholic of course so there was a limited choice. Cromwell eventually talked the king into marrying Anne of Cleves. She looked OK from her portrait so a diplomat married her on Henry's behalf.

Int: So what went wrong?

B: Well, when she arrived Henry was horrified. He said that she looked like a horse and refused to have anything to do with her.

Int: So that was the end of Cromwell. And wife number six?

B: Catherine Parr? Well she had the good luck to outlive him.

■ SET E ■ PAGE 127

The British Royal Family

1 Excuse me madam, have you got a moment? What do you think of the Royal Family?

I think they're absolutely marvellous. I mean they are wonderful ambassadors for this country and represent everything that is good and great in Britain... not to mention all of the wonderful things they do for charity. And just think of all the tourists who come here because of the Royal Family. I really don't know what we would do without them. And the royal babies, I think it's just marvellous when a new one comes along, bless them.

2 Could you tell me what you think of the Royal Family?

The royal family. What that lot? I mean they cost the country millions don't they. There are so many of them too. Me, I'm unemployed and I have to live off fifty pounds a week but they've got millions and we still have to pay them. If I had my way I'd...

3 And you, sir? Do you think the Royal Family does a good job?

To tell you the truth I don't think much about them at all. They're alright I suppose. They do a pretty good job... I wouldn't like to be one, I mean, they're always in the public eye aren't they?

4 Would you mind telling me what you think of the Royal Family?

They're harmless, I suppose. The only thing is they're a bit out of date. They don't really mean much in the modern world, do they? It's not like in the old days when the king led his armies into battle. They're not much use but at least we know what we've got though. We don't have the circus the Americans have every four years when they elect a new president. That really makes me sick. The only real thing I don't agree with is that we have to pay for them. Taxpayers I mean. After all they're rich enough already.

UNIT 15

■ SET C ■ PAGE 133

What a bargain!

Liz Balfour: Well, here we are. Let me open the door for you. Mind the step. Here's the sitting room.

Miranda Short: Wow, it's really big isn't it?

Liz Balfour: Yes, but it could be really cosy. It needs to be re-decorated.

Miranda Short: Are all the rooms this large?

Liz Balfour: Yes, but you could always divide them.

Miranda Short: It's been empty quite a while, hasn't it?

Liz Balfour: Only a few weeks.

Miranda Short: It's freezing. What's that funny smell?

Liz Balfour: Oh, just a little damp.

Miranda Short: Do you think you could turn the central heating on?

Liz Balfour: Actually, it doesn't have central heating.

Miranda Short: Oh doesn't it? I thought it did.

Liz Balfour: No, I'm afraid not. But the previous owners had the roof and the attic restored. That's why it's such a bargain.

Miranda Short: Oh really. I thought it was because of the stories.

Liz Balfour: Those silly stories. You don't believe those, do you?

Miranda Short: But there had been a murder, hadn't there?

Liz Balfour: Oh yes. But...

Miranda Short: And the other people. They only stayed six weeks, didn't they?

Liz Balfour: I'm not terribly sure. Anyway, let's look at the rest of the house.. Let's begin with the cellar.

Miranda Short: OK then... as I'm here.

Liz Balfour: Watch out the door's a bit low. After you!

Miranda Short: Oh, thank you very much.

▥ SET D   ▥ PAGE 135

Vampire rumours

Interviewer: Would you mind if I asked you some questions?

Vampire: Not at all, dear boy; after all that's why we're here.

Interviewer: How long have you been, um a creature of the night?

Vampire: Since 1327, that's six hundred and seventy years.

Interviewer: Wow! And how were you 'born' if I can say that?

Vampire: Well I happened to knock at the door of Count Dracula's castle in the middle of the night.

Interviewer: Why, were you lost?

Vampire: Not at all, I was a tax collector for the King at that time – so you can see I've always been a blood sucker, ha-ha. Anyway I wanted to catch the count at home.

Interviewer: I see. So he bit you and that was that.

Vampire: Quite.

Interviewer: Now I'd like to turn to your powers. Is it true that you can fly through the air?

Vampire: Absolute nonsense.

Interviewer: And what about being scared of crosses.

Vampire: Rubbish too – they have absolutely no effect on us.

Interviewer: But what are you scared of then? I mean, what about the sun.

Vampire: Ah yes, that's true. We have to be tucked up in our coffins before the first rays of sun otherwise we burn.

Interviewer: We have heard, do excuse me for bringing this up, that the only way to kill a vampire is with a wooden stake through the heart.

Vampire: Oh dear you have been watching too many horror films – but actually you are right.

Interviewer: And what about garlic, you know, protecting people against the attention of vampires?

Vampire: It depends on the tastes of the vampire – my English cousins can't stand foreign food, but I love a bit of garlic or paprika myself!

Interviewer: And finally, is being a vampire lonely?

Vampire: Not really, I have my family. There's my wife Lucretia and my boy Vlad Junior…

Interviewer: Your wife… Where did you meet her?

Vampire: In Rome back in 1430 I think. Anyway, there she was across the room. I had to have her. It was love at first bite…

Acknowledgements

We are grateful to the following for permission to reproduce copyright material:

BBC Enterprises Ltd for an extract from *Tricky Business* by Glenn Kinsey; Fourth Estate for an extract *Dog Eat Dog* by Wensley Clarkson. Copyright © 1990; The Macmillan Press Ltd for an extract from *The Macmillan Encyclopedia*. © Market House Books Ltd; Random Century Group on behalf of the authors Sting and John-Pierre Dutilleux for an adapted extract from *Jungle Stories: The Fight for the Amazon*. Published by Barrie & Jenkins; Random House Inc for extracts from 'Credo' in *All I Really Need to Know I Learned in Kindergarten* by Robert Fulghum. Copyright © 1986, 1988 by Robert Fulghum. Reprinted by permission of Villiard Books, a division of Random House; Rex Features for modified extract from the article 'Stopped Because I was a Black in a White Porsche' by John Kay and Matthew Cole in *The Sun* 6.6.90; J. Walter Thompson Co Ltd for an extract from BAA 'Body Language' advertisement; Solo Syndications Ltd for adapted extracts from the articles 'When all is not what it seems' by Peter Martin in *YOU* Magazine/*Mail on Sunday* 18.1.87, 'Doctor put woman on Suicide Machine' by Jeremy Campbell in *Evening Standard* 6.6.90, 'Arnie . . .' in *Evening Standard* 7.1.92. We have also made reference to *Man After Man* by Dougal Dixon, published by Cassell PLC.

We are grateful to the following for their permission to reproduce copyright material and photographs:

Ancient Art & Architecture for page 121. Aquarius Picture Library for page 123. Associated Newspapers PLC for page 102 (bottom right). The Ashmolean Museum, Oxford. All rights reserved for page 142. John Birdsall Photography for pages 61 (middle), 80, 81, 127 (bottom right). Martin Black for page 8 (right). Bridgeman Art Library/Belvoir Castle, Leicestershire for page 124, /Giraudon for page 55 (bottom), /D'Orsay, Paris for pages 55 (top), 56. Camera Press for page 122. J. Allan Cash Photo Library for page 74 (lower middle left) and 106. Redrawn with permission of Cassell PLC, from *Man After Man*, by Dougal Dixon for page 115. FAR SIDE Copyright CHRONICLE FEATURES, reprinted with permission. All rights reserved for page 110 (top left). Bruce Coleman Limited for pages 16 (bottom right), 48, 97 (bottom right). The Detroit News for page 44. The Environmental Picture Library/Irene R. Lengui for page 98 (main). Ronald Grant Archive for pages 16 (bottom middle), /Universal Studios for page 22–23. S&R Greenhill for pages 64, 127 (bottom left). Robert Harding Picture Library for pages 94, 97 (top right). H&R Photography for pages 42, 90. Hulton Deutsch Collection for pages 20, 118. The Image Bank/Werner Bokelberg for page 127 (top left), /John P. Kelly for page 12 (left), /Romilly Lockyer for page 74 (bottom), /G&M David De Lossy for page 61 (right), Mark Romanelli for page 68 (right middle). *The Independent* for page 102 (top). Kobal Collection for pages 16 (top middle, top right, bottom left), 46. Life File for page 61 (left), /Tim Fisher for page 127 (top right). London Regional Transport/Lovell Johns Limited for page 75. Longman Photo Unit for page 15. Lucasfilm Limited for page 24. Andrew Mann, redrawn with permission for page 8 (left). Simon Marsden for page 128. © Museum of London for page 74 (upper middle). Network Photographers/Jordan for page 68 (left). 19 Magazine for page 7. *The Observer* for page 82. The Photographers Library for page 74 (top left, lower middle right). Popperfoto for page 120. The Post Office for page 12 (right). Rex Features for pages 76, 98 (inset), 126. Solo Syndication/*Evening Standard* for page 84, /*Mail on Sunday* for page 60. Southampton City Art Gallery for page 38. Tony Stone Worldwide for pages 68 (middle), 72, 96, 97 (left). Syndication International 103 (middle, right), 119, / Mirror Group Newspapers for page 102 (bottom left). Tate Gallery Publications for page 138. Telegraph Colour Library for page 51, 74 (top right). Times Newspapers Limited for page 102 (middle). © Turner Entertainment Co. All rights reserved for page 16 (top left). THE FAR SIDE copyright 1985 UNIVERSAL PRESS SYNDICATE. Reprinted with permission. All rights reserved for page 110 (top right, bottom). Andrew Ward for pages 18–19. Zefa Picture Library (UK) Limited for page 68 (top, bottom right).

Picture on page 103 (left) taken from *Dog Eat Dog, Confessions of a Tabloid Journalist*, by Wensley Clarkson, published by Fourth Estates, London. Editor of book trying to contact author in California, but permission granted in author's absence.

We have been unable to trace the copyright owner of pictures on page 30, and would be grateful for any information to enable us to do so.

Special thanks to Barclaycard and Mr Ray Harryhausen.

Illustrated by Tim Archbold, Mike Bambury, Philip Bannister, Kathy Baxendale, Gary Benfield, John Bradley, Mark Draisey, Susannah English, David Frankland, Nick Harris, Rod Holt, Bizz Hull, Carol Kemp, Frances Lloyd, Bethan Matthews, Alan McGowan, Lester Meachem, Andrew Oliver, Pantelis Palios, Chris Pavely, Stephen Player, Johnathan Satchell, Taurus Graphics, Bee Willey and Gary Wing.

Cover illustration by Paul Wearing.

Author's Acknowledgements

The author would like to thank the following people:

- Richard Acklam (International House, London), Virginia Garcia (Sociedade Brasileira de Cultura Inglesa, Rio de Janeiro, Brazil), Hara Garoufalia-Middle (UK), Sandra Klapsis (Omiros School, Greece), Cristina Leito (Sociedade Brasileira de Cultura Inglesa, Rio de Janeiro, Brazil), Tim Oswald (International House, Lisbon, Portugal), Jeremy Page (UK), Sandra Possas (Sociedade Brasileira de Cultura Inglesa, Rio de Janeiro, Brazil), Carol Skinner (Greece), Emer Wall (Greece), Tricia Watts (UK) for piloting and reporting on the materials.

- My students, colleagues and teacher trainees at International House, London who have helped to develop the approaches used in this course.

- The team at Longman: Judith Cunningham and Howard Middle (publishers), Nicola Witt (designer), Delia Greenall and Thérèse Tobin (editors), Hilary Fletcher (art editor), Penny Faux (audio visual producer), Donna Wright (production controller) and Alison Derbyshire (publishing assistant) for their unstinting support and commitment.